I Don't Want Delilah, I Need You!

What a Woman Needs to Know and
What a Man Needs to Understand

I DON'T WANT DELILAH, I NEED YOU!

WHAT A WOMAN NEEDS TO KNOW AND
WHAT A MAN NEEDS TO UNDERSTAND

by
Bishop Eddie L. Long

BETHANYHOUSE
Minneapolis, Minnesota

Published by Bethany House Publishers
A Ministry of Bethany Fellowship International
11400 Hampshire Avenue South
Bloomington, Minnesota 55438
www.bethanyhouse.com

Printed in the United States of America by
Bethany Press International, Bloomington, Minnesota 55438

Library of Congress Catalog Number 00-687763

ISBN 1–57778–068–X

DEDICATION

To my beautiful, patient wife. You have inspired me to become the man God intended me to be. Delilah never had anything on you!

CONTENTS

FOREWORD

In every generation, God raises up mighty men and women to set things right in society. In the Old Testament, He sent Elijah to confront the nation of Israel with their sin and blast the prophets of Baal with His holy fire. In the New Testament, God sent Paul to preach the Gospel, stand before kings and idol worshippers, and confound them with powerful signs, wonders, and miracles. Today, He is sending men like Bishop Eddie L. Long to lead the Church in triumph over the forces of darkness and bring the saving, healing, delivering power of God to our nation and the world.

The Bible says in Isaiah 58:12, "And they that shall be of thee shall build the old waste places: thou shalt raise up the foundations of many generations; and thou shalt be called, The repairer of the breach, The restorer of paths to dwell in." This is a picture of what the Holy Spirit is accomplishing through the ministries of New Birth Missionary Baptist Church under the leadership of Bishop Long. The impact this man of God and his congregation have had on their city is phenomenal. And this book contains some of the life-changing truths God has given Bishop Long — truths and principles of the Word of God that will impact your life forever if you take them to heart and practice them.

You see, the key to the turning of a congregation, a city, a nation, and a world to God and to godly living is the divine restoration of families. Every pastor knows this. The pastor's heart in me breaks every time I counsel a person whose family has been ripped apart by divorce, a rebellious and wounded teenager whose father left shortly after she was born, or a young boy who is attempting to capture some sense of family in a gang. There is a holy rage that rises up in me every time I see the enemy destroy a life by destroying a family.

The wisdom Bishop Long imparts to us in this book is part of God's answer to my holy rage and to our nation's moral sickness. In these pages we hear God calling and teaching the husband to be the spiritual head of his home, to protect and love his wife as Jesus does His Church, to guard his family from every enemy, to raise his children in the counsel and admonition of the Lord, and to take full responsibility for everything that goes on under the roof he provides. There is the challenge to a wife to trust in the husband God has given her, to know what brings him down and what enables him to soar like an eagle, to work with him and not against him, and to maintain God's peace in the home. And there is a strong message to young people, single people, and single parents regarding relationships with the opposite sex and the power of sexual purity — before and after marriage. No matter where you are now, this book gives you a place to start.

When you have the people of God operating on this level of faith, love, and wisdom, you are seeing homes through which God can accomplish something phenomenal in this earth.

For these reasons, I am honored and excited to write this foreword. My friend, Bishop Long, is a hard-hitting pastor who tells it like it is. I've watched him share divine pearls of wisdom that have escalated him to unrivaled heights as a man of God. Therefore, I am proud to present to some and introduce to others a uniquely crafted ministry for couples who are ready to add more life to their years together.

T. D. Jakes, Sr.

INTRODUCTION:

CATCH A GLIMPSE OF GOD'S HIGHER PURPOSE

Most of us have what we *need*. I've traveled this nation extensively in recent years and have encountered very few instances in which people are lacking the things they need. Most people have food, water, shelter, and sufficient clothing to survive.

The state most of us are in today is a state of *want*. To a great extent, our state of want is related to our family life and to our marriages. We don't have everything we *want* to have. Those who are single very often want to be married. Those who are married very often do not have the quality of marriage they want. They want a better marriage, a different marriage.

We are miserable because of our wants, not our needs. And that may not be a bad state to be in! It can be the start of something good.

The important question to ask when you are making decisions and taking actions based upon your wants is this: Am I going after what it is that *God* wants? If you are unhappy with the way things are, make sure you are desiring a change that is in keeping with God's plan for you. Those who pursue God's plan will succeed in getting something better. Those who pursue their own plan in rebellion to God's plan will eventually fail miserably.

YOUR MARRIAGE MUST REFLECT GOD'S TRUTH

The Bible is not offered to man as a suggestion, a philosophy, or an opinion. It is given to man as truth. And because it is God's truth, God commands us to obey it. He doesn't ask us to study it and decide for ourselves if this is the way we want to live. He doesn't offer His truth to us as an alternative. He *commands* us to follow His plan if we are to be His people and to enjoy the blessings He wants to bestow upon us.

The Bible begins, **In the beginning God created...** (Genesis 1:1). God made you. He created you with a specific plan and purpose in mind. He made you who you are, including the sex you are. He established an order for you to live in relationship with other people, including an order for marriage.

It requires faith to believe what God has established as truth and to follow God's truth in obedience. We are never going to understand completely all of God's reasons for His creation. The Bible tells us plainly that God's ways are higher than our ways. (See Isaiah 55:9.) God also tells us that without faith, we will find it impossible to please Him. (See Hebrews 11:6.)

Throughout history, God says to His people, including us in the Church today, "You don't have to prove that I exist, just know that I AM."

God is the great originator and initiator of His own plan. We do not have the privilege to dispute it or to change it. We only have the privilege to choose to obey it and be blessed by it through our faith and obedience.

False systems of theology and philosophy begin with man and seek a way to God. But the Bible starts with God and is the story of God reaching out to man. If we are to accept what He offers to us, which is His unconditional love and forgiveness, then we must respond to Him with two things: our faithful and steadfast obedience and our thanksgiving and praise. When we do, we have peace and fulfillment in our lives. If we attempt to live according to our own ways, we have anything but peace and fulfillment!

THIS ENTIRE BOOK IS FOR *YOU* — EVEN IF YOU ARE SINGLE

This book is about God's plan — God's truth — for the marriage relationship and the family. Every chapter in it is for *you*. Don't assume that just because one chapter seems to be aimed at men or another toward women that you should skip over that chapter. There's information about God's plan, God's truth, that you need to know. We each must get the *whole* truth about God's plan for marriage if we truly are going to have marriages that are stronger and more fulfilling.

This book is not only for married people or for those who are planning to be married in the immediate future. It is for people who are divorced or separated. It is also for single people. Very often when a single person sees a book like this, aimed primarily at the marriage relationship, he or she thinks, "I'm single, so this doesn't have anything for me." Nothing could be further from the truth!

If you aren't married today, the likelihood is that you someday will be, or that you at least want to be married someday. Every unmarried person — child, teen, single adult, divorced adult — and *every* married person needs to have a proper understanding of the role of a man and a woman in marriage. If you're young and have never been married, you need to know this so you can prepare to be married. You need to get yourself ready to live out a godly marriage.

If you're divorced or separated, you need to have a new understanding so you'll know what went wrong. Then you won't continue to make the same mistakes in the future that you made in the past.

Even if you're single and you believe God has called you to be single, you still need to have this information. There are married people who are going to share various problems with you, and you need to have a good answer from God's Word to share with them.

An understanding of God's plan for the marriage relationship is vital for our witness as the Church to an unbelieving world. The first place a nonbeliever looks to see if the Church "works" is to the family. They look at a believer's relationship with their spouse, children, or other family members even before they look at that believer's personal integrity or moral stance. Why? Because how you relate to your spouse, your children, and your parents is going to reveal to that person how you are going to relate to them should they become a believer too.

This message is for everyone.

And it's a message that is for NOW.

CHAPTER 1

SAMSON AND DELILAH: AN "OUT OF ORDER" RELATIONSHIP

We often learn as much in life from examples of what "not to do" as we learn from examples of what "to do." Certainly that is the case with Samson and Delilah. Of all the stories in the Bible, the story of Samson and Delilah is a story of a failed relationship between a man and a woman. We can learn many things from this story — truths that are vital to our understanding of God's plan for marriage and for family.

The story of Samson and Delilah is not a love story — at least not from Delilah's side. Rather, it is a story rooted in two very different motivations. From Samson's side of the story, we read about love. But from Delilah's side, we see a much different motive at work.

And it came to pass afterward, that he loved a woman in the valley of Sorek, whose name was Delilah.

And the lords of the Philistines came up unto her, and said unto her, Entice him, and see

> **wherein his great strength lieth, and by what**
> **means we may prevail against him, that we may**
> **bind him to afflict him: and we will give thee**
> **every one of us eleven hundred pieces of silver.**
>
> **Judges 16:4,5**

Samson was drawn to Delilah by love. His was a sexual attraction, but apparently his feelings were not limited to sex. The Bible says that Samson "loved" a woman named Delilah. In previous instances when Samson was with a woman, we find that he "went in unto her," a description that implies sex only. There are other ways the Bible describes a sex-only relationship — a man might "lie" with a woman or "know" a woman, and those are descriptions of a sexual relationship. None of them describe Samson and Delilah. In this case, the word love is used.

What about Delilah? Did she love Samson? There's no evidence in the Bible that she did.

DELILAH WAS SAMSON'S ENEMY

Delilah was approached by the Philistine leaders, and the implication is that she was a woman who could be enticed by money. She could be "bought" — her services could be gained for a fee. In at least one other incident, Samson had been found with a prostitute, whom the Bible calls a harlot. (See Judges 16:1.) Delilah may have been a prostitute, although the word harlot is not used to describe her. In any case, in the end she does what she does with Samson for *money*. In today's money, she was promised about five thousand dollars if she would do what was asked of her.

Delilah not only agreed with the Philistine lords that she would be with Samson for money, but she would see that Samson was somehow tied up so that physical harm could be done to him. The plot was clearly spelled out to her. She didn't act in ignorance. She knew that the end of this story would be pain and perhaps even death for Samson. She was a co-conspirator with a group of Philistine men who were Samson's enemies. In fact, she very likely was a Philistine woman herself. In her heart of hearts, Samson was *her* enemy.

Can a woman have a sexual relationship with a man even though her heart isn't in it, even though she considers him to be an enemy? Of course! It happens all the time.

Do some women — apart from prostitutes — manipulate men for money using sexual appeal and sexual relationships? Of course! It's not at all uncommon. Even wives sometimes resort to sexual manipulation to get what they want materially and financially from their husbands. Perhaps the most insidious manipulation of all is when a Christian woman will attempt to use Scripture to get a man to do what she wants!

Do some women know that what they are doing will bring great harm to the men they are manipulating? Of course they do. Even knowing it will bring harm, they continue to manipulate.

Do men want to be manipulated, used, and hurt? Of course not. No man wants a Delilah! Yet men are victims of Delilahs all the time.

NOBODY'S PERFECT, BUT...

Many women will claim they never want to be like Delilah, and they would reject any suggestion that they have anything in common with her — yet they often do as Delilah did. But before we get too hard on either Samson or Delilah, we must recognize that *neither* of these people was perfect. Samson wasn't a completely innocent victim. In this story, one person wasn't necessarily all that much "better" than the other. Neither are we perfect as men and women today. No person is without sin. Romans 3:23 makes it very clear: **For all have sinned, and come short of the glory of God.**

Every story has two sides, and there are nearly always negatives on each side. That's reality. And that's one of the great things about the Bible — it's *real*. It's about real people, it's about real problems, it's about real flaws, and it's about a real God. Some of the greatest heroes of the Bible start out as imperfect men — in fact, some of them have great flaws and make terrible mistakes.

Why should we study imperfect people? Because of what *God* does in their lives! Time and again we see that if the imperfect heroes and heroines of the Bible submit themselves to God and His purposes, God uses them to accomplish great things. The good news for all of us is that God can take an imperfect man or an imperfect woman and use that person for His purposes. He can change the human heart. He can bring about His perfection using imperfect vessels — including you and me.

MANIPULATION

In any marriage relationship, manipulation is a deadly force. It may not be the woman who is manipulating — it may be the man. The manipulation may not actually be focused on the relationship — it may be a mutual manipulation related to outside sources. Even so, that manipulation will spill over into the relationship and kill it.

The most deadly manipulation of all is when one or both partners in a relationship seek to manipulate God's truth and twist it to suit their own purposes, justify their sin in the process, and bring about a "disorder" that is contrary to God's plan.

The Bible gives us a clear example of manipulation in the way Delilah related to Samson:

> **And Delilah said to Samson, Tell me, I pray thee, wherein thy great strength lieth, and wherewith thou mightest be bound to afflict thee.**
>
> **And Samson said unto her, If they bind me with seven green withs that were never dried, then shall I be weak, and be as another man.**
>
> **Then the lords of the Philistines brought up to her seven green withs which had not been dried, and she bound him with them.**
>
> **Now there were men lying in wait, abiding with her in the chamber. And she said unto him, The Philistines be upon thee, Samson. And he brake**

the withs, as a thread of tow is broken when it toucheth the fire. So his strength was not known.

Judges 16:6-9

Samson and Delilah were playing a little game. Samson didn't know it was a deadly game and that he was the intended victim. He was just playing a little love game, perhaps a sexual game. Delilah, on the other hand, was going for high stakes. She was out to get her five thousand dollars. Samson knew full well that seven freshly cut vines, or sapling branches, weren't going to hold him. He was toying with her. She was toying with him.

Any time we begin to "toy" with another person, trying to get that person to do what we want for *our* purposes and not for God's best, we are manipulating. We are treating a person as if that person were a "thing" — a puppet whose strings we pull to get our way. When we treat a person as a thing rather than as a special creation of God, we are acting outside God's boundaries. Delilah is into manipulation, and her purposes are 100 percent contrary to God's plan and purpose.

For his part, Samson is manipulating by lying. He doesn't tell Delilah the truth. He's being deceitful, perhaps to see what sexual games Delilah might come up with once he's all "tied up." He's not out to hurt Delilah, but neither is he acting in a godly way.

Then what happens?

And Delilah said unto Samson, Behold, thou hast mocked me, and told me lies: now tell me, I pray thee, wherewith thou mightest be bound.

And he said unto her, If they bind me fast with new ropes that never were occupied, then shall I be weak, and be as another man.

Delilah therefore took new ropes, and bound him therewith, and said unto him, The Philistines be upon thee, Samson. And there were liers in wait abiding in the chamber. And he brake them from off his arms like a thread.

Judges 16:10-12

If there's ever an example in the Bible of love blinding a person, it's the story of Samson!

Most men probably would have said, "Hey, this girl is working with my enemies. She doesn't love me. She's using me!" But a man in love doesn't think that way. He justifies what happens so that his sweetheart comes out pure and innocent. A man in love says, "It's just a coincidence those Philistines showed up. But hey, I have everything in control. After all, Delilah warned me that these guys were attacking. She's on my side."

So Samson agrees to play the game a little longer. Big mistake! It's *always* a mistake when we refuse to face facts and confront the enemy for who he is and what he is doing in our lives. People justify the facts all the time to suit their own purposes. They rarely face up to the fact that the devil is trying to destroy them and is using certain people for his ends.

WAKE UP!

Samson was accustomed to the Philistines being after him. Right before this story of Samson and Delilah we read how Samson had gone to see a harlot in Gaza. While he was there, the Gazites surrounded him in an ambush, intending to kill him when he emerged from the harlot's house in the morning. But at midnight Samson had arisen, gone out, took the two doors of the gate along with their posts, and carted off the doors, posts, bar, and all. (See Judges 16:1-3.)

Not only was Samson accustomed to the Philistines being in hot pursuit of him, but he was accustomed to defeating them at whatever trick they plotted against him. He may not have perceived that this instance with Delilah was anything other than the fact that the Philistines had discovered his whereabouts and were after him once again. However, he probably didn't associate Delilah with his Philistine enemies.

How many people are like Samson today? They know in their minds that the devil is after them, but they are tricked by people again and again because they do not see that the devil uses people, and that some people are willingly used by the devil. They fail to associate the people's actions as *really* being the actions of the devil against them.

Wake up, Samson! Wake up, man who is reading this book! Wake up, woman who is reading this book! There's an enemy out there who is putting his greatest effort to the destruction of your marriage relationship, your family, and your witness as individuals and as a family in this world today. There's an enemy out to destroy your effectiveness for God!

Samson becomes a victim once again. This time he allows Delilah to bind him up with new ropes. Again, he has to contend with men who are hiding nearby, lying in wait to destroy him. Again, Delilah sounds the alarm. Again, Samson breaks the new ropes off his arms as if they were cotton sewing thread.

Does Samson wake up and smell the coffee this time? No. He is truly blinded by his love for this manipulating woman.

> **And Delilah said unto Samson, Hitherto thou hast mocked me, and told me lies: tell me wherewith thou mightest be bound. And he said unto her, If thou weavest the seven locks of my head with the web.**
>
> **And she fastened it with the pin, and said unto him, The Philistines be upon thee, Samson. And he awaked out of his sleep, and went away with the pin of the beam, and with the web.**
>
> **Judges 16:13,14**

Samson makes a big mistake in round three of this tug-of-war with Delilah. He gets his hair involved in his "games." Delilah accused Samson of lying to her, which he clearly knows he has. Samson knows the source of his strength and the manifestation of that strength in his life. So he moves a little closer to the truth.

Manipulators always use accusation at some point in their bid to get what they want. If someone begins accusing you, sit up and pay attention. Even if the accusation is accurate, the *use* of accusation is not godly behavior when it is in the context of trying to get you to do what *they* want you to do.

You can certainly point out to your accusers how their behavior is opposite of what the Word of God commands, but you are always wise to let your statement end there. A person's obedience to God should never be linked to what you desire, but rather, your obedience to God's Word should be because God commands certain behaviors. Obedience to *God* is the right thing.

Delilah doesn't say, "You shouldn't lie, Samson. It's not right to lie before God." No — she says, "You've lied to me and in doing that, you have mocked me. Now, tell me the truth."

TESTING THE LIMITS

Samson should have known clearly at this point that there was no way it was mere coincidence that he had been bound up three times by Delilah, that three times the Philistines just happened to be hanging around waiting to destroy him. He may very well have come to regard this as a game he was playing, not only with Delilah, but with the Philistines and with himself. He may have been trying to prove something about his own strength, his own manhood, his own ability to test the limits of God's patience with him, or to see how *close* he could come to the edge without crossing over the line.

Do men and women do that today? All the time!

How many people do you know — including yourself — who engage in behaviors they know aren't right before God? They hope that just this one time, or in just this one case, God will turn the other way and perhaps not see their sin. If He sees it, perhaps He will ignore it. It doesn't happen! God, Who sees all and knows all, hates sin in every form. And every sin has a consequence, perhaps now or perhaps later, but always.

Even after this third experience, Samson comes back for more:

> **And she said unto him, How canst thou say, I love thee, when thine heart is not with me? thou hast mocked me these three times, and hast not told me wherein thy great strength lieth.**
>
> **And it came to pass, when she pressed him daily with her words, and urged him, so that his soul was vexed unto death;**
>
> **That he told her all his heart, and said unto her, There hath not come a razor upon mine head; for I have been a Nazarite unto God from my mother's womb: if I be shaven, then my strength will go from me, and I shall become weak, and be like any other man.**
>
> **Judges 16:15-17**

Notice what Delilah did. She not only accused Samson of lying to her and making fun of her, but she "pressed him daily with her words." She began a relentless campaign to find out what she wanted to know so she could use that information against Samson.

BE CAREFUL WHAT YOU SAY!

There are some things we don't need to talk about, and especially to people who don't know God, don't want to know God, and show no interest in God. Those who are outside the Body of Christ are under the influence of the enemy of our souls. We must love them, pray for them, and witness to them about Jesus Christ, but we are putting ourselves in danger when we begin to share with them the deep spiritual truths of God's Word and the way He works in the human heart. Jesus taught,

Give not that which is holy unto the dogs, neither cast ye your pearls before swine, lest they trample them under their feet, and turn again and rend you.

Matthew 7:6

Those who aren't saved and filled with God's Holy Spirit don't know how to love you fully. They shouldn't be trusted with your most vulnerable secrets and confessions. Guard your tongue. Prove who is trustworthy in your life. Watch for signs of spiritual maturity in the other person before you talk to them about the deep working of God in your life.

Samson told Delilah the very source of his strength before God. He trusted his whole life to his enemy, and she used that information against him:

And when Delilah saw that he had told her all his heart, she sent and called for the lords of the Philistines, saying, Come up this once, for he hath shown me all his heart. Then the lords of the Philistines came up unto her, and brought money in their hand.

And she made him sleep upon her knees; and she called for a man, and she caused him to shave off the seven locks of his head; and she began to afflict him, and his strength went from him.

And she said, The Philistines be upon thee, Samson. And he awoke out of his sleep, and said, I will go out as at other times before, and shake myself. And he wist not that the Lord was departed from him.

But the Philistines took him, and put out his eyes, and brought him down to Gaza, and bound him with fetters of brass; and he did grind in the prison house.

Judges 16:18-21

Delilah was a good "reader" of people. This time she knew with certainty that Samson had told her the truth. She sent for her money. She had Samson's head shaved. And sure enough, Samson fell victim to his enemies.

One of the saddest lines in this story is this: **he wist not that the Lord was departed from him** (Judges 16:20). Samson apparently thought he would always have the great manifestation of God's power in his life. He may not have believed that if his hair was cut, God's supernatural strength would depart from him. Samson may have come to believe,

I may not be AS strong, but I will still be stronger than my enemies. Not so. In telling Delilah his secret and having his hair shaved off, Samson was saying to God, "You can't trust me with Your power." And whom God can't trust, God doesn't use.

In the end, God's Word remained true and Samson's ideas proved to be lies. When his head was shaved, Samson lost his strength. He was bound and shackled by the ungodly Philistines, subject to being used by them for *their* purposes. He lost his vision when his eyes were gouged out, and he became a slave to an evil enemy.

WHAT NO MAN WANTS

In some respects, Delilah was everything a man wants. First, she was a woman Samson loved, and every man desires a woman to love. Men are made to love their helpmates. Men have a strong need for love. Second, Delilah was no doubt willing to "make love." Every man wants a willing sex partner. Third, Delilah gave Samson a willing and comfortable lap in which to lay his head and tell his secrets. He trusted her. And every man wants a woman who provides a place for him to rest his head, tell his secrets, and place his trust.

But there are things about Delilah that NO man wants! No man wants a woman who will connive with other men against him. No man wants a manipulative woman. No man wants a woman who will project herself as something she isn't. No man wants a woman who nags him day and night for what she wants. No man wants a woman who will betray him. There was far more about Delilah that was undesirable than desirable.

Christian wives, your husbands don't want Delilah — not really — and especially if they can have you! They need *you* to love them, comfort them, and hear their secrets. But beyond that, they need you to be godly women whom they can trust with all of themselves.

Before we can truly have a right relationship with another person, however, we need to gain a proper understanding of who we are in the Lord. From that, we can determine who we are to be to each other in a marriage relationship. Until our identity is in focus, our relationship never will be.

CHAPTER 2

KNOW WHO YOU ARE

S amson knew who he was. There wasn't any doubt. He was a Nazarite, which meant he was a man who had been consecrated and set apart for God's purposes. He had lived as a Nazarite — a devoted and consecrated life — from the time he was born.

As a Nazarite, Samson lived under a vow to God never to cut his hair, drink wine or strong drink, or eat unclean foods. This was the definition God gave to the Nazarite vow. (See Judges 13:4,5.) Samson had lived according to this vow from his birth.

Samson also knew his purpose in life. Even before his birth, an angel had told his mother and father that Samson had been chosen by God to **begin to deliver Israel out of the hand of the Philistines** (Judges 13:5).

VOWS MUST NOT BE TAKEN LIGHTLY

Vows are meant to be kept. They are not meant to be made and then forgotten. Part of keeping a vow means to renew it often. A vow covered Samson's life from his birth, but we have no record that

Samson willingly kept that vow alive in his heart by renewing it frequently.

If you have made a vow to the Lord or before the Lord, renew it often. If you have set yourself apart as a holy man or woman of God to do those things God has predestined for your life, then you must repeatedly consecrate yourself to the Lord. Remind yourself of your position before God and His purpose for your life. Keep at the forefront of your awareness the vows you have made with regard to your wife or husband and the raising of your children in a godly home.

If you have failed to keep a vow you have made to God, ask for His forgiveness. Say again to the Lord, "I make a vow to live holy for You in the name of Jesus!"

CALLED TO BE A FORCE FOR EMANCIPATION

Samson was called to be an emancipator and bring about the deliverance of his people. At the time, the Israelites were under the yoke of the Philistines. Samson brought them deliverance and was the judge of the Israelites for twenty years.

Christian men and women today are called to be a force of emancipation, to bring about the deliverance of people from the yoke of Satan. We are called to bring people out of darkness into the light, out of bondage into freedom in Christ Jesus.

Emancipators Must Be Strong. To be an emancipator, a man must first be *strong*. One of the foremost things God has ordained for all men is that they be strong.

The kind of strength God has ordained is a strength of spirit, mind, and emotions — not just a physical strength. God is looking for men who want to be strong, who are not afraid of developing their strength. That strength is going to be manifested as courage, boldness, steadfastness, and in powerful spiritual warfare.

First and foremost, *God* desires this strength of men, but so do *women* desire this strength of men. Women often say, "I'm looking for a man who can be strong." They aren't talking about a man who can bench press heavyweights. They are talking about a man who is strong in spirit, mind, and heart — someone they can trust to be immovable in the face of a stormy circumstance, someone who can stand up for what is right and fight for what is right if necessary, someone who will defend his wife and children and home, someone who will fight and defeat the devil in the spiritual realm.

Every woman I know wants a man who is secure within himself because he is secure in God. Such a man knows who he is, says what he means to say, means what he says, walks the way he talks, and above all, walks tall and boldly in the Lord.

Growing Into Strength. Men don't emerge as strong emancipators overnight. They aren't born strong emancipators. Just as a little baby boy has to grow up into the fullness of his physical manhood and strength, so a man must grow up in the Lord to become strong in Christ Jesus. He has to put away childish issues. As the apostle Paul wrote,

> **When I was a child, I spake as a child, I understood as a child, I thought as a child: but when I became a man, I put away childish things.**
>
> **1 Corinthians 13:11**

Samson didn't just emerge one day as a one-man fighting machine for the Israelites. He grew into that strength and understanding.

One of the first occasions in which Samson experienced the mighty power of God flowing through him was when he went to the vineyards of Timnath, which were in Philistine territory. A young lion "roared against" him, and the Bible tells us that the Spirit of the Lord came mightily upon Samson. He tore that lion as if it had been a little goat kid. He did this bare-handed, no doubt ringing the lion's neck and pulling its joints apart. (See Judges 14:5,6.)

Just as Samson had to grow up into his strength and his understanding that he was a chosen emancipator for his people, so men today must grow up in their understanding of who they are in Christ and what God has called them to be and to do.

SAMSON DIDN'T HAVE THE BIG PICTURE

Samson knew he was to be an emancipator of his people, but for some reason, he never seemed to get the "big picture" of that call. He just went from one fairly minor situation to the next, reacting to situations and circumstances instead of predetermining what needed to be done.

We each need to pray that God will give us the big picture for our lives and for our marriages and families. Imagine what your marriage will be like ten years from now, thirty years from now, and fifty years from now. Make a lifelong decision about your marriage and then get the lifelong picture. Come to the understanding that 90 percent of the things you think are important to you today will *not* be important to you four or five years from now. Do not let yourself make lifetime decisions based on temporary appeal or fleeting importance. If you do, you will be building failure into your life.

Most shortsighted decisions are rooted in feelings, not in rational thinking. Emotional decisions may allow you to do some things that are good, but they do not allow you to do what is best. There is a big gap between what is *good* and what is *best*.

The person who is ruled by their emotions is a person who is going to be blown off course by the least little trouble. Such a person is highly unstable. One day they feel one way, the next day they feel another way. There's no counting on such a person, there's no trusting that kind of person.

It's *good* to have emotions, to know how to express them properly and use them for their intended use — which is to motivate us to confront evil and pursue good. Emotions give us that extra burst of strength to do what we know is right.

I praise God for emotions. They've saved me from harm on more than one occasion. I recall a time when I was in middle school and I had to walk home each day by a house that had two Dobermans locked up in chains. I'd stop and bark at those dogs and then run from them because I knew their chains would stop them. That was a little game I played with those dogs. But…one day I came up to where those Dobermans lived and I found that they had been set free. And believe me, they were free *indeed!* I ran faster than I've ever run in my life. I wished at that moment I had been in the Olympics, because there would have been no doubt that I would have captured the gold medal. The emotion of fear gave me a boost of energy that sent me flying to safety.

It is also *good* to be able to think intuitively and emotionally. That's the way most women think. But it's *bad* to be ruled by emotions, to be governed by them, or to make them the guiding force of one's life. A person who operates according to undisciplined and unbridled emotions is like a cork bobbing on the water, constantly reacting to what other people do and say. Such a person is very prone to entering the "blame game," justifying their actions by their feelings and on the basis of how others *made* them feel. Don't get into that! God won't honor it.

If you continue to live by emotions and lusts, rather than by the Word of God, you will develop a "victim" mind-set. You will see yourself as subject to the whims and actions of others. That's not the destiny God is calling you to have. His desire for you is to be *more than a conqueror* — a victorious person in Christ Jesus, a person who sets their face like a flint toward what is right. You remain immovable and unshakable in faith and receive all God has for you.

Learn to take charge of your emotions and to discipline them — not eliminate them, but discipline them. Your emotions must always be subjected to what God says, what God requires, and what God is desiring to do.

The emotion Samson felt for Delilah was an emotion that was not governed by what Samson knew to be true before God. He made decisions out of a lust of the flesh and a lust of the eyes, not with emotions that were under control and a mind that was subject to God's Word.

Disciplining yourself about what you see and what you think is very important. In fact, it is vital to your having a satisfying and joyous marriage. If you are always in a reactionary mode to your senses and your feelings, you will always be questioning yourself, others, and your marriage. You will live in a state of not trusting your spouse or children. You will be prone to unhealthy jealousy and anger.

When this happens, you are reacting to life just like that cork that bobs up and down, being tossed to and fro by the waves of the ocean. Even if you know who you are, you are not acting like it. And whatever God's plan is for your life, you are probably missing most of it.

YOU WERE BORN TO SOLVE A PROBLEM

Every person who has ever been born was born to solve a problem. It may not have been a problem from their perspective, but it was a problem from God's perspective.

When you isolate and define problems in your life, face up to the fact that you were born to solve those problems, so that they would cease to be problems for your children and future generations. You were born to bring a degree of deliverance to this earth. And in that way, you are no different than Samson. He was born to be an emancipator, and so are you!

In many ways, you are called to emancipate your own children from the parenting errors *your* parents made with you. You are called to emancipate yourself, your family, and ultimately your heirs from the generational sins of your ancestors.

YOU WERE BORN TO CONFRONT YOUR SOCIETY

Part of the problem you were created to solve is the problem of society as a whole. When we are silent to the crime, corruption, and lack of morals in our world today, we are just as guilty as if we were participants. It's time that we speak up, even if we cause some dissension. Jesus said:

> **Suppose ye that I am come to give peace on earth? I tell you, Nay; but rather division:**
>
> **For from henceforth there shall be five in one house divided, three against two, and two against three.**
>
> **The father shall be divided against the son, and the son against the father; the mother against the daughter, and the daughter against the mother; the mother in law against her daughter in law, and the daughter in law against her mother in law.**
>
> Luke 12:51-53

Jesus wasn't seeking trouble for trouble's sake. But He knew that the truth of God is sharper than any two-edged sword in separating the truth from the lie, the good from the bad. (See Hebrews 4:12.) And when you confront a society with their evil and immorality, even some of your family members may come after you!

An old proverb states that the ruin of a nation begins in the homes of its people. It's so true! The ruin of our nation is not going to occur because of what happens in our government. Any problem you can name today in our society had its start in the home. Even the problems we have in government come from a home problem, because all of our political leaders grew up in homes. Our churches are made up of families — any church you can name is a composite of "homes."

Not only is our family life the foremost witness to the world, it is also the key to our receiving greater blessings from God. A person once said, "The church meets, but it has no keys." That person was referring to Jesus' promise that He would give "the keys to the kingdom" to His followers.

A church is just a group of people who have come together to perform a little ritual unless that church has the "keys" to unlock the power of God, which in turn brings conviction, blessing, and growth. It is only when the home is in order, and then collectively the "home" of the church is in order, that God will say to His people, "You're mature enough now to handle the keys of the kingdom."

If homes are out of order, then the church that is the collective "group" of those homes is also going to be out of order. God will not bless the marriage, the family, or the church that is operating apart from His plan. Your church can never be stronger than the families who comprise it and support it. If husbands are acting in an unchristlike manner at home, their church is not going to be a church that submits to God. The chain of authority has been broken.

We have countless churches across our nation that are gatherings of people assembled under cross-topped steeples, but they are people who have no respect for the order of God. They have no right to expect God to anoint what He has not ordained. Indeed, God will not anoint their gathering as long as they choose to willfully function apart from His order.

WHAT WILL HAPPEN?

What are the consequences to us if we don't come to grips with the problems that are in our marriages and families? What will happen if we don't emancipate ourselves from the devil's plan and seek out God's plan? What will happen if we don't confront our society and go against the grain of the times to live the way God wants us to live?

The third chapter of Isaiah tells us what happens when a nation falls under the judgment of God because the godly people in it have followed the "ways of the world." In this passage we find that God removes that which strengthens a nation.

> **For, behold, the Lord, the Lord of hosts, doth take away from Jerusalem and from Judah the stay and the staff, the whole stay of bread, and the whole stay of water,**
>
> **The mighty man, and the man of war, the judge, and the prophet, and the prudent, and the ancient....**
>
> **And I will give children to be their princes, and babes shall rule over them.**
>
> **Isaiah 3:1,2,4**

The "stay and the staff" are gone. This is referring to the stock and the store, the basics for living and making a living. In many neighborhoods today we find this lack. There are no stores, no thriving businesses. There are pitifully few resources.

The mighty men are gone. Without the mighty men, a society collapses. Women do not have husbands and children do not have fathers to care for them and protect them. In many segments of our society, we find the "mighty men" missing — killed on the streets, locked up in prison, and running away from their God-given responsibilities. The society they have left behind is falling apart.

When women begin to run households and have the responsibility not only of nurturing and training their children, but also providing for their children, the plan of God has been set aside. Children begin to rebel. In their rebellion, they oppress their elders. This isn't to say that single mothers are bad mothers. Not at all! It's to say that they have been forced to survive in a situation that is *not* God's plan for them! It takes a man to instill authority and to maintain it.

My wife often gets frustrated when she feels that our sons don't obey her. She'll say, "I have to tell them over and over and over to do things. You only have to tell them once." She's right. I'm the man, I'm the father, I'm the leader who is responsible and therefore in authority. Now, I have to say what I say and do what I do with love, but when the father speaks, things happen. That's simply the way God made us to function. It has nothing to do with shortchanging women. It has everything to do with men standing up and fulfilling the role God has given them to fulfill.

Mature adult rulers are missing. God puts in their place "children to be their princes" (Isaiah 3:4).

These may be adult people, but they have a childish state of mind and a strong impulse to selfishness.

On the one hand, you'll find many neighborhoods today in which the youth are ruling. Gangs are in control. Women, children, and the elderly walk in fear. Teachers are afraid to discipline students for fear that a gun will be pulled on them. Shopkeepers put up iron bars because they fear burglaries.

On the other hand, we also find many areas of our society in which adults are simply acting like children. The little girl or boy who pouted when they didn't get their way as a child is now a spouse who gives their mate the silent treatment when things don't go the way they want them to go. The child who is wounded and bitter because they come from a divorced home carries bitter self-centeredness from the playground to the corporation or even the government. We look at the decisions they make and the laws they pass and we ask, "How did so much ignorance join itself together?"

Believe me, if I was dependent upon the government to protect me and provide for me, I'd be plenty nervous! That doesn't mean all politicians are bad or stupid, but when you look behind closed doors at the process that runs most government agencies, bureaucracies, businesses, and organizations of any kind, you'll feel as if you're watching a whole lot of boys and girls dressed up and trying to act like adults. The result of their actions is very often an oppressed society, group, corporation, or people.

> **When I was a child, I spake as a child, I understood as a child, I thought as a child: but when I became a man, I put away childish things.**
>
> **1 Corinthians 13:11**

Now before God is going to reverse this trend for the hurting people in our world, we are going to have to return to doing things His way. Then and only then are we going to find that the decisions being made are godly and unselfish. Mighty men will again take charge of their families and provide for them as they should. The resources will begin to flow and neighborhoods will become stable and prosperous.

The good news is that it's within our grasp to do this. We *can* start living according to God's plan and doing things God's way. The trend can be reversed. We can come again into a state of blessing if we are obedient to God's commandments and His order for society.

In Deuteronomy 28, we also find a sharp line between the blessings of living in obedience to God's plan and the curses of living in disobedience. Read that chapter. You'll be both convicted and blessed by it. I believe you'll draw the same conclusion I draw from it — I'd much rather be living in a place where people are obedient to God's plan!

HAVE A STRATEGY!

NOW is the time – not only for us to face up to who we are to be in Christ and what the consequences are for not living according to God's plan, but also for us to develop a plan, a strategy for getting back on track with God's plan. Samson *knew* who he was called to be, but he never developed a strategy for *implementing* God's call on his life. He never made a commitment to do *only* what God desired for him to do, or to be *only* what God desired for him to be.

We each must come to a point of resolution within ourselves and with our spouse about our marriage. We must decide we *will be God's people and live according to God's plan.*

Develop a strategy for how you are going to improve your marriage and family life. I used to love to watch the boxer, Mohammed Ali, call a round. He would say, for example, "And in the fourth round I'm going to take him out." He would call the round because he had a strategy to his fighting. He knew what he planned to do in the first round, and then in the second round, and so forth. His strategy called for him to have his opponent so tired and on the defensive that he could knock him out in the round he predicted.

Now we can get prideful if we think we will be able to accomplish our goals or defeat the devil by a certain date on our personal calendars. What I do recommend, however, is that we have a strategy for growth, improvement, development, and expansion.

Samson had no strategy for his life. He went from one crisis to the next, from one situation to another. Many people are like that. And if that is the way you are operating your life, a Delilah can come along at any point and trip you up.

GOD'S ULTIMATE PURPOSE

Finally, we must know that the ultimate purpose of God for setting the family into place and establishing a divine order for man, woman, and child, is so the world might be redeemed. The reason we are to be emancipators, the reason we are to solve a problem, the reason we are to confront our society is so that we, our marriages, our families, and our world might be redeemed by God. Everything God has put into place is so the world might see His image and come to be in full fellowship with Him.

God did not create the order of man, woman, and child to punish one part of His creation or to create any kind of inequality or imbalance. The exact opposite is true! He made man, woman, and child to work together in spirit — equal in spirit, but different in function — that the world might function in harmony, and that all of His creation might live in fulfillment because each is enjoying a loving relationship with Him.

God's plan is always for your good, now and through all eternity. It is always a plan for your complete redemption and your everlasting wholeness. And when you are redeemed, when you have been saved and cleansed by the blood of Jesus, He begins to show you who you are and give you the keys of the kingdom to live who you are in this world – especially in your marriage and family.

CHAPTER 3

SPIRITUAL EQUALITY AND DIFFERENT FUNCTIONS

B efore we have any hope of getting our relationships in order, we first must gain an understanding about who we are as human beings, and particularly as men and women.

The most important aspect of our humanity is the fact that we are spiritual creatures, made in the image of God, Who is spirit. In Genesis 1:26,27 we read about God's spiritual order for men, women, and children:

> **And God said, Let us make man in our image, after our likeness: and let them have dominion over the fish of the sea, and over the fowl of the air, and over the cattle, and over all the earth, and over every creeping thing that creepeth upon the earth.**

> **So God created man in his own image, in the image of God created he him; male and female created he them.**

These verses in the first chapter of Genesis tell us God created a "spirit man." Any reference to the male gender by itself refers to the spirit of all mankind — male and female. In the spirit realm male and female are created equal in essence. But in the natural realm, God created the sexes to function differently.

This is a critical concept to understanding yourself and your marriage: *Men and women are equal in spiritual essence, but different in practical function.*

Because there is a difference in function within the physical, material, natural world in which we live, we have the two words "male" and "female." Because there is no difference in the spirit realm, we have one word for the human race, "man." Because the Scripture says "man" was made in God's image and "man" has dominion or power and authority over the earth, we know that male and female *together* are to have dominion.

DOMINION TOGETHER

The understanding we must gain in the Body of Christ is that the only way we can take dominion over all of creation is if we, male and female, come together in spirit — no longer warring against one another, but warring together against our common enemy, the devil.

Paul said in Ephesians 6:12, **We wrestle not against flesh and blood, but against principalities, against powers, against the rulers of the darkness of this world, against spiritual wickedness in high places.** Our fight is not with each other — male versus female — and neither is it to be with other human beings. Our battle is in the spirit realm, which is where we are *supposed* to have dominion! We are not supposed to be defeated by the devil and his demons. We are created by God to have dominion, to be victorious, to be on top.

Somehow in the Body of Christ we have been tripped up into thinking that we must fight *people* in high places. No! We are to fight the demonic powers that control and influence people. When we win in that arena and truly take dominion, we don't have to worry about people. We are victorious.

The Church should have graduated by now from "he said, she said, and so-and-so said." That is not our battlefield. We must elevate ourselves and move into the heavenly sphere, saying to one another, "Child, you are fightin' the wrong fight!" We need to lift ourselves up and esteem ourselves higher so we can come together, male and female, united in spirit to destroy the devil's attempts to bring the image of God to shame.

The devil goes to the core. He doesn't play sideshow games. He's out to destroy our society by hitting us at the very image of God. Until Christian men and women come together in spirit, there is no example to the world of how men and women can be united — equal in spirit, yet different in function — taking dominion together over all that is evil. It's up to us to lead the way in our society — if we don't lead, we won't succeed.

THE UNISEX FACTOR

James Dobson has written about what he describes as a unisex society. A unisex society is one in which men and women seek to become one in function. The lines between masculinity and femininity are blurred greatly.

The warning is this: In thousands of years of human history, and in the thousands of cultures that have existed in human history, there were only a few that made the mistake of trying to become unisex, and the ones that did quickly died. Not one unisex society has ever survived more than a few years.

A unisex society is one in which women demand to be equal to men in *function*, not essence. Any time the women of a society say, "I can be a man and still be a woman," they are fooling themselves.

Those who have studied unisex societies note these three characteristics:

In a unisex society, the women reject their children and kill their babies in their desire to be more like men. Take another look at the abortion rate in our nation and you'll have to agree that we are very much moving into a unisex society on this front.

In a unisex society, the women move into and seek to dominate in the marketplace. We already have statistics that tell us that 51 percent of all for-wages jobs are held by women.

Now please understand that I'm not saying a woman can't get an education or have a job. Many godly women work and successfully keep their homes together. The danger lies in those who enter the marketplace thinking that their measure of success in life is competing with men, and to some extent, competing with the man in their own home to become the foremost breadwinner in the family.

Working women routinely complain that their husbands don't help enough with the "details" of running a home. Man wasn't created with a capacity for doing those details — including seeing that they need to be done or feeling responsible to do them! A man needs a woman to fill in those blanks of his life. He also needs to feel as if he is doing his part well by providing for and protecting his wife and family.

If you take away the support of the "details" given by a helpmate, much less ask the man to do those details for the woman, or if you take away the man's sense of providing for and protecting his family, you emasculate the man. In the process, he'll lose his vision. He'll lose his warrior spirit. He'll cease being the best example and leader he can be.

In a unisex society, women go "on the make" for men. The women seek out casual sexual relationships and become the aggressors in pursuit of men. I admit to you that I got very frustrated when my older son was still living with us and he would sit by the phone and wait for a woman to call him.

I'd say to him, "Well, who do you want to talk to?"

He'd give me a name.

"Why don't you call her?"

"No," he'd say, "I'm not going to do the calling. She has to call me."

If my son wasn't working and couldn't put gasoline into the car, I'd say to him, "You're not using my car this weekend."

He'd respond, "That's all right. My date is picking me up."

I'd say, "And I'm not giving you money to pay for the date."

He'd say, "No problem. She's paying."

I knew in my heart every time he came back with those statements, *that girl he's dating is headed for a heartache!*

Women, teach your daughter that she doesn't need to solicit. Teach her to be a queen and not lower her standards. Teach her to wait for a man who is a king, a priest, a mentor, a warrior, a man who has a big heart filled with love. Don't let her get hooked up with a lazy man. Don't allow her to become the aggressor after a man. Teach her to say to a young man, "This is the last time I'm going to let you call me unless you learn how to talk to a lady, because I am a lady. Then I'll let you call me again."

Assure your daughter that if she will remain a queen, the men who will come after her are much more likely to be kings!

When my wife and I go out as a family, our son Jared is my wife's date and our daughter Taylor is my date. Jared takes my wife by the hand, opens the car door for her, and makes sure she is strapped into her seat belt. I take Taylor and strap her into the back seat and make sure she's comfortable. Now Taylor is only three years old as I'm writing this book, but let me assure you, if your son plans to marry my daughter, he had better come prepared to treat her like a queen, because she's going to have a high standard. That young man who marries my daughter is going to have to live up to the reputation established by Taylor's daddy!

Start "dating" your children when going out together as a family. Show your children by your example how their future dates and mates should treat them. Challenge them to live to a high standard and to claim only godly excellence for their lives.

A man is always looking for a challenge. When he finds a woman who will challenge him to be his best, he'll respect her and want her all the more. I see young women out with guys and I want to say to the women, "Why did you allow yourself to be seen with that guy? His shirt is hanging out, his sneakers have holes in them, his cap is on backwards. Why didn't you tell him when he came to your door, 'Do you think I'm going out with you the way you look? Get yourself together and then come back.'"

A girl may think she'll never see that guy again, but let me assure you, she'll either see him again and he'll have his act together, or the word will get around and someone else will show up at her door with his act together. She doesn't have to settle for a man who has such a low opinion of himself.

The man who comes across a woman who challenges the best in him may feel a little low at first. He may walk away and sulk for awhile. The fact is, the warrior spirit in him hasn't encountered this kind of prey before! But the next thing you know, that man will be in the barbershop and trying on some new clothes because he's going to come back around to try to see what makes this woman tick. She's got his interest. She's caused him to set his sights higher.

THE KEY TO FULFILLMENT

Your inner peace lies in your discovery of who you are — who God created you to be and what God has planned for you. Once you know that, you *will* succeed — for there's nobody who can beat you at being you!

You have been created by God to be His beloved child. You have been called by God to be in right relationship with Him through Jesus Christ, to be forgiven of your sins, filled with the Holy Spirit, and blessed with an abundance that is overflowing. (See John 10:10.)

As a believer in Christ Jesus, you are called to be an active member of the Church — offering your praise, your resources, your time, your talents, and your energy to further the kingdom of God. You are personally called to be a witness for Christ to your spouse and to your children. As a family, you are called to be a witness for Christ in your church and in your community.

You have been given unique gifts and talents which you are to use for God's glory. You have been given an ability to communicate, to express, and to create. You are to use those abilities to minister to others — your spouse, your children, fellow believers, friends, colleagues, and lost souls.

You have been created to be either a man or a woman, and if you are married, you have been called to be a husband or a wife. If you have children, you have been called to be a parent. You have a God-given purpose in living! Your peace, satisfaction, and fulfillment will come in living out God's purpose for you.

The path to misery is in trying to live out someone else's purpose. Women who are trying to take on the purpose of men are going to be miserable. Wives who try to take on the purpose of husbands, and mothers who try to take on the purpose of fathers, are going to be miserable. Those who try to "live out" the purposes or expectations of other people — rather than to live out the purposes of God for their individual lives — are going to be miserable.

Discover who you are in Christ and then BE that person!

CHAPTER 4

MAN: MORE THAN A RHINOCEROS SPIRIT

An amazing thing happens when a man becomes a man. I'm not talking about being a *male*. I'm talking about becoming a man of character, grace, and mercy. This is a man who can be a judge and an elder sitting in the city gate to bring peace and resolution of problems.

When a man becomes who he truly is to be as a man, a woman has a much greater possibility of becoming all that she can be as a woman. This automatically means that children have a much greater potential as children to grow up and move in a greater dimension of God.

God created physical man first, and in doing so, He made man the foundation of His human creation. He then pulled woman out of man, and finally took the child from the woman. The foundation for life on this earth lies with the man.

Throughout history you'll find that there is an overall plot of the devil to "get the man." When you study this in the Bible, you'll find examples from Genesis to Revelation. The main attempt of the devil is not to destroy the woman, but to destroy the man. Why? In part, because the devil knows that if he gets the man, he also gets the woman and the child.

The spirit of the rhinoceros is a picture of 150 percent commitment. Once the rhino makes up his mind to do something or go somewhere, there is no stopping him. And the key to his purpose and well-being is to be on the move accomplishing what he wants to accomplish.

Most men, however, do not truly understand who God created them to be or the role they are to fulfill in relationship to their wives and children. They are suffering an identity crisis. This identity crisis has arisen to a great extent because men are drawing their identity from the wrong source. They are looking to the world instead of the Word for a definition of who they are and how they are to act.

One of my Christian sisters wisely reminded me recently that the Christian life calls for a man and a woman to live a life that is totally *against* what most of the world is doing. If you read the popular magazines found at our grocery checkout counters, you'll find a lifestyle depicted that is the opposite of what is proclaimed in God's Word.

These worldly sources present a totally distorted view of what it means to be masculine. Masculinity is not found in lifting weights or building up muscles. It is not tied to athletics or the ability to run seven miles every morning. It isn't found in drinking more than the next guy, owning a fancier car, or bragging to other men about how many girlfriends you have or how much money you make. The man who has such a definition of masculinity is a man who has drawn that image from the world he has observed around him, not from the truth of God's Word.

It's time we return to what the Creator
says about His creation!

GOD'S DEFINITION OF MAN

God has a much different definition of what it means to be a truly masculine man. Four of the traits we find repeatedly in the Word of God are these:

• Man is called to be a king.

• Man is called to be a warrior.

• Man is called to be a mentor.

• Man is called to have a heart of love.

MAN IS CALLED TO BE A KING

Man is called to be a king over a domain, which is generally his work and his family. Within his domain of influence, man is to rule by making godly decisions, solving problems in a godly manner, and executing a godly vision.

A man's vision will determine what kind of "king" he is. A godly king will rule a godly kingdom. An ungodly man, with a false vision, will most likely be a despot or a dangerous dictator. A large part of a man being "king" is related to the vision God gives him for his life. A worldly man's decisions are based upon the vision he has of the world. But a godly man will have a heavenly vision for the home, the community, and the world in which he finds himself.

Men Have the Ability to See the Big Picture. Men have been created to see the "big picture." That's one of the reasons most men are so bad at small talk. That's also the reason why most men are oblivious to details and minor troubles.

A man will conclude that everything is all right with his sleeping children if they are quiet and in bed. A woman, however, will go repeatedly to check on her children, making sure the blankets are pulled up around them and they are sleeping peacefully. A man figures that if a child isn't hollering, he's doing okay! (That's one of the reasons men need women — babies might die if men were responsible for attending to the detailed needs of helpless infants!)

There's a balance to man's visionary trait, and that is the "detail orientation" that a woman has. A woman has an ability to see the small differences, the small factors. Women have an uncanny and God-given ability to notice "the least little thing."

When I check on our babies, I'm just looking to see if they are crying or not. My wife, however, goes over to the crib and makes sure the baby's covered, doesn't need changing, and every detail is okay. When looking at a house, I just tell my wife whether I like it or not. She looks at the ceiling to see if anything's peeling, which might indicate a leak in the roof, and especially what kind of carpet or flooring is laid to see if they are the colors that will go with our furniture.

Men rarely zero in on the details of a woman's life. A man generally can't tell you the color of the hat his wife wore to church last Sunday, or the color of her dress, or how high her heels were. He sees her as a total picture. He responds to her not just by the way she looks but by the way she walks, talks, laughs, and relates to him. A man doesn't know if the floor has been mopped or the laundry has been done. He only knows that he either feels welcome and "at home," or he doesn't.

A woman, in contrast, struggles to see the big picture of a man's life. She knows all of the details of his appearance and behavior, and she is likely to point out his slightest flaws. She knows her husband didn't take out the trash, doesn't make as much as the husband down the block, or that he didn't pick up the right brand name at the grocery store. But most women do not have the big picture of who their men are in the world or what they can be to the church or community as a whole. Their focus is narrower, tighter, and in many ways, more practical.

This isn't to say that some men aren't more detail-oriented than others, or that some women aren't more visionary than others. But by and large, men tend to be visionary and women tend to be absorbed by detail. As we saw earlier, Samson was concerned about the defeat of the Philistines as a whole so Israel might live in peace and freedom, but Delilah was concerned about whether she should use green saplings or new ropes to bind Samson.

Visionaries Get Battered. In many ways, men are being "beaten up" continually today in our culture, and perhaps especially so in the black community. They are being hammered on the details. "This isn't right and that isn't being done. You aren't accomplishing this and you aren't doing that." A visionary person who is constantly confronted with details is going to feel both talked down to and trodden down in spirit.

The truth of God in this is: The devil knows that if he can stop the visionary, he can kill the people. The devil knows that if he can put a stop to those who see God's big picture, he can enslave the entire population by leaving them to fight about "sins" related to details.

A Clear Vision of Kingship. When a man gains a clear vision, he comes into a new understanding of *himself* — created by God to be a "king" under the authority of the King of kings, Jesus Christ; *God* — the ultimate sovereign King of the universe, the Almighty Holy One; and *the relationship man is to have with God* — ruling his kingdom but under the rule of his King.

A man who gets this vision and gains this understanding moves from being a fool who doesn't know who he is or where he is going to being a man who rightfully sees himself as a king on this earth who is expected to take dominion over a portion of God's kingdom.

There was a time when I didn't have a strong vision from God for my life. People who know me now can't believe that was ever true, but people who knew me as a child can't believe that I am who I am now! I was the class clown as a child, a C — and often a D — student. I was a "write-off" in most people's minds. But there's a wonderful passage of Scripture that depicts my life to me:

> **Hath not God made foolish the wisdom of this world?**
>
> **For after that in the wisdom of God the world by wisdom knew not God, it pleased God by the foolishness of preaching to save them that believe.**
>
> **Because the foolishness of God is wiser than men; and the weakness of God is stronger than men.**
>
> **For ye see your calling, brethren, how that not many wise men after the flesh, not many mighty, not many noble, are called:**
>
> **But God hath chosen the foolish things of the world to confound the wise; and God hath chosen the weak things of the world to confound the things which are mighty.**
>
> **1 Corinthians 1:20,21,25-27**

Every time someone calls a man a fool, it's time to look out. God may just be getting ready to confound the wise with that "foolish" man!

The challenge every man faces is to get his definition and his vision from God. That's the way to move from being a fool to being wise. It is also the key to being used in God's kingdom and to ruling wisely over the domain God gives to you.

Visionaries Can't Keep Quiet. When a man truly has a vision from God, he can't stay quiet about it. When he gets on fire with something he believes in his heart, he can't shut up. He sees the mountain he is going to climb or the building he is going to build and he tells everyone he knows, "I see it, I see it." Man has the ability to communicate the big picture. He's excited about communicating the vision. And his enthusiasm is contagious.

Visions Are Meant to Be Implemented. Visions are given to kings so they might turn those visions — things unseen in the natural world — into reality, something which can be seen and experienced. When a man sees something that he wants to achieve, he sets in motion everything around him. Kings and visionaries are created to be *starters.*

A vision doesn't turn into a reality without a price. A vision bears a price tag — of faith in God, of hard work, of trust on a daily basis, of working with other people. A vision is a burden that a man carries in his heart. The vision is something he knows *must* be done, and it is something the man *wants* to do. Yet just knowing and wanting doesn't turn a vision into reality. There's money to be raised, work to be done, and people to be brought on board to help with the vision. In addition, sometimes laws need to be changed, problems need to be solved, and obstacles need to be overcome. A man not only is a starter, but he is the one who bears the responsibility for being a *finisher.*

One of the things that is so frustrating for many women today is that Satan has been allowed to put out the vision of their men. I have said it often to men's groups: It's very difficult for women to follow a parked car. If a woman is linked to a man who has no vision, she is frustrated because she has nowhere to focus her energies and her abilities.

A Loss Can Be Regained. What happens if a man loses his vision? What happens if he loses his kingdom and ceases to function as a king? All is not lost — as long as that man hasn't lost his inner vision of his relationship with God! *A man who has lost everything but still has God is a man who has the potential to regain what he has lost.*

Some men get themselves into a position of so much inner pain and so much pressure that they think they're dead on the inside. They don't have any hope that they might live without pain and pressure. The fact is, however, they are still alive.

No doubt Samson had moments when he thought he might as well be dead after the Philistines had captured him and put out his eyes. There he was, grinding at a millstone for them day after day, week after week, month after month. He was living in a prison house, and we can only imagine the conditions he lived under during that time in history. He was blind, led from place to place by people who were his enemies. Death may have seemed like a relief to Samson.

But Samson wasn't dead. He was alive.

God's call hadn't left his life. It remained.

Samson may have lost his strength and his eyesight, but that loss was not necessarily forever. God was still moving in him. God hadn't released him from his purpose. And over time, Samson's hair grew back. His strength began to return, in his spirit and in his body. His vision returned — not his eyesight, but his inner spiritual vision.

If you have lost your vision and your kingdom — or if you have never had vision or a kingdom — don't give up hope. Ask God to renew your strength. Spend time with the Lord and in His Word, building up your faith in Him and regaining your understanding of who God made you to be. Allow God to renew your vision within you. Trust Him to give you back the kingdom He intends for you to rule under His authority!

MAN IS CALLED
TO BE A WARRIOR

God gave man a fighting spirit. If you take that spirit away from a man, he becomes paralyzed and doesn't do anything. He sits, mopes, and rots. I like to refer to this fighting spirit as a "rhinoceros spirit," which means men are intended by God to be tenacious and willing to do whatever it takes to get a job done. They'll run through walls if need be. In the spirit realm, they have skin that's two inches thick and can't be penetrated.

One of the elders in my church told me one day that he had watched a rhinoceros in a zoo that had ground off its own horn. In essence, it had "wimpified" itself because it was no longer in a position to be a warrior or to engage in a fight. Because it was caged and held captive, the rhino's spirit was broken.

There are women who, upon "capturing" their men, put them in a zoo of sorts, attempting to restrain them on every front. What they don't realize is that they are putting their rhinoceros-spirited men in a position where they will become wimps. In their desire for everything to be perfect for their men, these women are actually weakening their men.

A Christian woman must realize that if she wants a true man of God as her husband, she must *not* want certain things to die in him or for him to stop doing certain things. He was given a warrior spirit by God and that spirit must not be quenched.

Warriors Gravitate to Warriors. Few men are stupid enough to engage in a battle on their own. They might fight a man one-on-one, but they rarely take on a whole group of men in a battle. Warriors gravitate to other warriors. In a negative way, we see this in the gangs that roam many inner-city neighborhoods. We see this tendency in the sports teams that engage millions of men as "weekend warriors."

Every man I know is looking for someone to cry, "Charge!" Men will move locations, switch jobs, and even change religions because they see a leader of men crying, "Charge! Let's take this territory. Let's move in and rule!" Men all over this world are looking for someone to say, "Let's go, brother. Lock your arm with mine and let's conquer this thing."

The key is this: *Make certain the person you gravitate toward out of your warrior spirit is a leader worth following.* Look at his life. Look to see if his walk matches up to his talk. Look at the whole of what he says and does. You can get in big trouble if you are marching behind the wrong leader into the wrong battle.

Warriors Can Be Stubborn. To be a warrior is a great thing, but to be a warrior who thinks he is invincible or always right is a very dangerous thing. A man's warrior nature can make him hardheaded and crusty. Men have a hard time admitting they're wrong. Women know this, and so do men. That old rhinoceros hide can be tough. Men don't take kindly to people telling them they have made a mistake or they are wrong.

On the one hand, this is a matter of pride. A warrior must always guard against being ruled by pride. On the other hand, many women don't know how to tell their men they are on the verge of error or they have erred. The wrong thing to do is to come at a man like a sergeant snapping a private to attention, or to come at a man rolling your eyes in disgust or pointing your finger. A woman who comes at a man like that is only going to bring out his impulse to fight. She's going to awaken the raging warrior in him rather than help the noble warrior in him to fight the right battles in the right ways.

Dominance Does Not Mean Abuse. One of the problems we have is that some men have understood in their spirits that they were created by God to dominate, to have authority, to be "mighty men," but they didn't understand the full plan of God — that they were to be godly in all of their actions. The result has been that some men have sought to lord over women. They have disrespected women, beat women, raped women, and abused women.

Men must come to understand that women are equal to them in spiritual essence, only different from them in function. Women are to be loved, cherished, protected, held in high esteem, and made to be the queen who sits on the adjacent throne.

I have no tolerance for domestic abuse. I have told the women in my church that if their husbands get out of line, send us their work address and their daily schedule and we'll go after their men. There's no excuse whatsoever for violence or sexual, physical, or emotional abuse of women and children in the home. If a woman is in an abusive relationship, she needs to get out of that situation, separate herself physically from the problem, and let her church work on her behalf.

It doesn't matter what a woman does or doesn't do that might trigger anger in a man. It is the responsibility of a man to deal with his anger in a godly way. He must deal with his authority issues so he doesn't feel he has to bully his way around his home.

MAN IS CALLED TO BE A MENTOR

God made men to be role models, to give guidance to others, and to "help" others reach their potential. A man has an ability to see a problem and to *know* it is a problem. It is therefore a vital part of man's role to point out to others when errors are being made and to put a stop to them.

Lots of people blame Eve for the sinful world we live in. I don't. I blame Adam far more than I blame Eve, because Adam failed in his role as a mentor. Eve was deceived when she listened to a talking snake, and she ate the fruit of a forbidden tree when he tempted her to give it a try. Women are curious. They are spiritually sensitive. They focus on the beautiful. All of these traits are wonderful when they are manifested in a godly way.

Women generally want to experience all that God has for them. Remember that the devil tempted Eve by convincing her she would be like God if she ate of this fruit. Eve wanted to be like God! God was wonderful to her — He was her Creator, her Friend, her Source of all supply. She responded to the devil as women respond — intuitively, instinctively, spiritually. But she made a mistake. If she had truly wanted to be like God, she would have been 100 percent obedient *to* God. Eve was a woman who was 90 percent right, but the 10 percent that was wrong was WAY wrong.

Notice, however, that nothing happened in the wake of Eve's sin. The whole world wasn't immediately plunged into death. She wasn't expelled from the garden in an instant or thrust immediately away from Adam's sight.

The fact is, Adam could have corrected Eve's sin, because ultimately he was responsible for her. Adam had been given reason, objectivity, skepticism, rationality, authority, and responsibility. Adam could have, and should have, taken one look at what Eve was offering him and had the good sense to refuse it and lead her to repent of her deed before God. Instead, he joined her in eating the fruit. When Adam ate is when sin, guilt, and death took root. Adam failed to mentor. And if he had any doubt about what to do, he should have gone to *his* mentor — God, His Creator and Father.

The burden that rests on those who are higher on the authority ladder is that they have to report to the person above them. In the case of a man and wife, it's the man who has to report directly to God for the marriage. In a church, it's the pastor who has to report to God for the congregation. I've seen cases where an entire congregation was in error, but God had mercy because the pastor pleaded on their behalf and continued to do what was right. But let that pastor fall into error, and the entire church goes down.

The same thing happens in families. The wife and children can make all kinds of mistakes, but if the man will stand strong for what is right, the family survives and over time, it will heal and flourish. As head of his home, if a man ever has a question about when and how he should be a mentor, or what decision he should make as a mentor, he should go to *his* Mentor. He should ask God to show him what to do. He can turn to the Word of God and get wise counsel.

Many men abdicate the role of being a mentor to their children by saying to themselves, "Let my wife bring up the children." But God has called men to give guidance to their children, to teach them what it means to be a godly person and to have authority over what the children learn about right and wrong.

The devil is after men and after fathers because he knows that if he gets the man — the husband and the father — he is going to get the wife and the children. The devil isn't into bowling for spares. He wants to hit the kingpin and get a strike, knocking all ten pins down with one blow. He knows that if he can distract the man from mentoring and disciplining his children, he can destroy the entire family.

Mentoring has a twofold responsibility: *First, to see what is wrong and remedy it.* Men are called to be "repairers of the breach." They are to bind up those things in their life, marriage, and family that are broken. They are to join with others in binding up those things in their church and in their community that are in need of healing and restoration.

Second, to declare the truth of God. In this role, a man functions as a prophet. Men are called to speak the Word of God into their own lives, their marriages, the lives of their children, and their friends, neighborhood, and community. In sum, they are to speak God's truth to their entire sphere of involvement and influence. What you know to be true and good and right before God is what you are to speak. Then those things which you believe become those things which are your reality. As I stated earlier, a vision for what "can be" is of very little use unless it comes forth as a reality.

A number of years ago I found myself in a situation in which I had a vision for what was to be done. I knew there was a breach I was to repair, but I couldn't put that vision into words. Therefore, I couldn't express the vision to others and by so doing, bring forth those people who could help turn the vision into a reality. A vision burns in the heart, and if it goes unexpressed, that burning will gnaw at a man until he becomes frustrated and miserable.

To be a prophet in the home is to speak God's Word and to live out God's Word in such a way that God's Word is received and understood. It is to hold to God's highest standards, and in holding to them, to be a role model for excellence and purity of character.

Be encouraged in this — your witness for Christ will not return void. The "word" that you express to someone else about Christ's love and forgiveness and strength will not return void. (See Isaiah 55:11.)

MAN IS CALLED TO HAVE A HEART OF LOVE

Men are called to express the feelings and love of their hearts. So many men have given this role to women, thinking that to show love is to show weakness. Nothing could be further from the truth. **God so loved the world, that he gave his only begotten Son** (John 3:16). God shows His love. Man has been created to show love, to express affection and give praise, and to give hugs and kisses to his wife and children.

The apostle Paul gave a great challenge to men in Ephesians 5:25-32:

> **Husbands, love your wives, even as Christ also loved the church, and gave himself for it;**
>
> **That he might sanctify and cleanse it with the washing of water by the word,**
>
> **That he might present it to himself a glorious church, not having spot, or wrinkle, or any such thing; but that it should be holy and without blemish.**
>
> **So ought men to love their wives as their own bodies. He that loveth his wife loveth himself.**

> **For no man ever yet hated his own flesh; but nourisheth and cherisheth it, even as the Lord the church:**
>
> **For we are members of his body, of his flesh, and of his bones.**
>
> **For this cause shall a man leave his father and mother, and shall be joined unto his wife, and they two shall be one flesh.**
>
> **This is a great mystery: but I speak concerning Christ and the church.**

This is a word of destiny for the family and a word of power for the Church. It is a liberating word for women and most definitely a word of hope for children. But in many ways, this is a tough word for men.

Why is this a difficult word for men? Because when a man comes to an understanding that he is to love his wife *as Christ loved the Church,* he is brought face to face with the fact that he is called to "die" for his wife just as Jesus died for the Church. This is not a physical death, for Jesus' death on the cross never needs to be repeated. This is a death to *self.* It is to die to self-centeredness, selfishness, and pride. It is to die to me-first and me-only plans.

When I finally faced this, I discovered once again how difficult it is to face *myself* most of all, to conquer myself that others around me will live. But I also find that the life I give for others brings a greater life back to me.

Men are called to give of themselves sacrificially to their wives. And the truth is, if a man never dies to his own selfish desires and begins to give to his wife, she can never fulfill her purpose or truly be in submission to him. She may be submissive, but her submission will be incomplete and ineffective until he loves her as Christ loved the Church — sacrificially, continually, and with a love that is equal to his love for himself.

God's role for husbands is to provide leadership, not to make demands. Man is to lead by being an example of service and love, just as Jesus Christ served the Church and offered His own life out of His love for mankind.

A man need only ask God to expand his capacity to love his wife and children. If he thinks his love for his wife has died, he should start treating her *as if* he loved her, and he is likely to find his love for her rekindled. No love is beyond God's ability to resurrect it. A man must choose to love his children and learn to show affection toward them.

The Bible says this about the ministry of John the Baptist:

And he shall go before him in the spirit and power of Elias, to turn the hearts of the fathers to the children, and the disobedient to the wisdom of the just; to make ready a people prepared for the Lord.

Luke 1:17

God's desire today is that fathers be turned toward their children, and that the Church bring the disobedient into the wisdom of the just — so that we, too, might be a people who are fully prepared for all the blessings of the Lord's presence and power in our midst. The Lord is calling you as a father to turn again to your children with a heart filled with love.

OPERATING ON ALL FOUR CYLINDERS

When a man operates on all four cylinders as a King, Warrior, Mentor, and with a Heart of Love, he truly moves into the fullness of his God-created manhood. He fulfills the purpose for which he was made. And — he is *unstoppable!* He truly can get all things done that God has ordained for him to do.

If you want to know how to succeed as a man, choose to do things God's way.

Choose to be a godly king with a vision.

Choose to be a godly warrior, fighting your battles first and foremost in the spiritual realm.

Choose to be a godly mentor, correcting and repairing what is wrong and giving a clear presentation of what is right.

Choose to be a loving husband and a loving father.

And then see what God will do through you!

CHAPTER 5

WOMAN: A MINISTER, NOT A DOORMAT

Most women today suffer from the same "identity crisis" that plagues men. They, too, are drawing their definitions of "womanhood" from the world. On the one hand, they are bombarded by women's magazines that tell them how to be beautiful, seductive, and manipulative. On the other hand, they are bombarded by women's movement advocates who tell them to be in competition with men and to take over the role of men whenever possible. Neither image is the one presented by the Word of God.

Much of what a woman is to be can be drawn from Genesis 2:21-23:

> And the Lord God caused a deep sleep to fall upon Adam, and he slept: and he took one of his ribs, and closed up the flesh instead thereof;
>
> And the rib, which the Lord God had taken from man, made he a woman, and brought her unto the man.
>
> And Adam said, This is now bone of my bones, and flesh of my flesh: she shall be called Woman, because she was taken out of Man.

This brief passage of Scripture tells us two great things about woman: *She is the bearer of new life and the nurturer of life.*

While she may not be the instigator of new life, a woman is the "bearer" of it. She is the vehicle or method through which new life comes into the world. A woman is a "wombed man." A woman has a womb, a man does not. A woman is female. "Fe" is the same root that gives rise to fetus. A woman is *female* because she has a womb in which she can carry a fetus. A woman has a womb in which she can incubate the seed which she receives from man. In her function as a potential mother, woman is a receiver, while man is a giver.

As a nurturer of life, a woman has been given breasts so she can nurse her children. In Bible times, mothers nursed their children for the first three to five years of their lives. One of the reasons children of that time were so obedient to their parents no doubt lies in the fact that children were kept close to the mother during these early formative years, relying on their mothers for nurture.

Being so close to their mother, children had the assurance and comfort of a parent who was nearby. They weren't "put off" on anyone else. They had access to their mothers and received training in how to think, act, and speak directly from them. By the time they were weaned, their personalities were formed and their allegiance to God and family were firmly in place.

As much as a man may desire to breastfeed his children, he cannot do it. A man was not created for this role. A woman is the one given the responsibility for this. It is part of the way she functions as a "cover" for her children.

We have made sexual identity a major issue in our world today, but God's viewpoint is a very simple one. He creates us for the purpose He intends for us. If He gave you a womb, He created you for the purpose of being a woman, with full potential to receive from a man and to carry a fetus within you.

Any time you have a doubt about your gender, look at what God gave you. If He gave you a womb, you are a woman, a female. It's very simple.

TAKEN FROM BONE, NOT EARTH

In many ways, woman is God's "better idea." God wasn't satisfied that He had made Adam alone. He pulled a woman out of him so that Adam could relate to her and be *better* than he was before.

God went into the dirt to make a man. He **formed man of the dust of the ground, and breathed into his nostrils the breath of life; and man became a living soul** (Genesis 2:7). In contrast, women were made from the bone of man. They were not pulled from the earth. That's one of the reasons why women just don't "look right" smoking, cursing, or covered with filth and grease and grime from doing all kinds of manual labor.

Men can look attractive when they are dirty. We see sweating, dirty, hardworking men on television all the time and we say to one another, "There's a macho guy." But women were not made from the earth. God made women to be lovely, gentle, clean, and beautiful on the inside and outside. They are to be strong in character — after all, they are made of *bone* — but they are to be soft in their outer demeanor and appearance.

In a society where little boys are exposed to grubby, cursing, dirty, cigarette-smoking, road construction worker women…is it any wonder they stop chasing women and start chasing men? There's a part of every little boy and every man that is missing — and it's the "softer side" that is gone. That side of a man is to be found in a woman.

I understand the reason some women have moved into careers and taken on jobs that men have traditionally held. A big part of the reason is that men either abandoned them, forcing them into these roles so they could support their children, or the men so abused these women when they were young girls and teens that they feel it's better to live without a social or spiritual covering than to live under a painful covering! They would rather fend for themselves than be abused or suffer the threat of being abandoned.

The blame doesn't fall solely on the woman for what's gone wrong in our society — just as the blame doesn't rest solely with Delilah for the demise of Samson. Much of the blame falls on men.

What God took out of man and put into woman, He never put back into man! That's why men and women seek each other. A woman is seeking the cover that she needs. A man is seeking that part of himself that was pulled out of him and wasn't put back into him. He is always in pursuit of his "missing bone."

I'm not at all bothered when men refer to their wives as "baby," because if we go back to the beginning, Eve is the only "baby" Adam ever had or ever would have. His wife was his only "begotten" one.

God gave woman to man to be his companion, friend, compassionate helper, lover, and an heir with him to the grace of creating new life on the earth. What a joy it is to bring in new life as husband and wife — both physically in the creation of children, and spiritually in the birthing of new believers.

GOD'S CALL TO INNER BEAUTY

One of the errors many women make is the mistake of thinking that physical beauty alone wins and keeps a man. That's a lie of the enemy.

Some men I know are married to very beautiful women and their lives are hell. The same for women. Some women I know are married to extremely handsome men and they are living in a terrible state.

On the other side of the coin, I know some handsome men who are married to wives who aren't all that physically attractive and they are in marital bliss. Some fine-looking women are married to ugly men and they seem utterly happy.

The point is — beauty on the outside does not mean beauty on the inside. A person can be beautiful in appearance and ugly in character. In the end, it's character that counts in a marriage.

Now not all beautiful people are ugly on the inside, and marriages between good-looking people aren't automatically headed for disaster! That isn't at all what I'm saying. What I'm saying is that you can never judge a marriage according to outer looks.

Peter advises women to have a beauty that emanates from their spirit. He says:

> **Whose adorning let it not be that outward adorning of plaiting the hair, and of wearing of gold, or of putting on of apparel;**
>
> **But let it be the hidden man of the heart, in that which is not corruptible, even the ornament of a meek and quiet spirit, which is in the sight of God of great price.**
>
> **For after this manner in the old time the holy women also, who trusted in God, adorned themselves, being in subjection unto their own husbands.**
>
> **1 Peter 3:3-5**

When a woman is operating out of her faith in God to submit, respect, and obey her husband, she has a quietness of spirit. The peace of God resides in her. And the stillness in her that is born of faith provides a connection to God that her husband sees and values, even if he doesn't know that is what he is seeing and valuing. He responds to it because that peace engulfs him and creates an environment for him in which he can become more open to God.

Peter tells the women that they can win their husbands with beauty — but not with outer cosmetics and clothing and face lifts and other kinds of "beauty secrets." Rather, wives will win their husbands with their inner confidence in God, and their meek and quiet spirits that reflect their faith.

WOMAN'S "TECHNICAL EXPERTISE"

Not only is man ultimately attracted to and influenced by a woman's inner character, but by her "technical expertise" in knowing how to create an outer environment of peace and beauty in which he can find rest.

Many men have a vision for what their family life and their marriage might be like. They have a knowledge of what needs to be fixed and they have an understanding of how things should be or could be. But they need a "repairer of the breach" alongside them, a woman who has the technical expertise to help turn that vision into a reality.

There's something that only a woman can do to turn a house into a home. She brings to that house a warmth, a smile. She brings an understanding of beauty, harmony, and peace. She knows how to turn a plant a certain way, hang a curtain a certain way, coordinate a schedule a certain way, fix a pot roast a certain way, and light a candle and arrange a bouquet of flowers a certain way. A man can build a house and he can know that he wants a home. But a woman knows *how* to create a home out of a house.

When a woman creates a place of peace and encouragement, she repairs many things in the hurting souls of her husband and her children. She provides a place, an environment, that is secure, nurturing, and comforting emotionally and spiritually.

WHAT DELILAH DID RIGHT

No one is 100 percent bad, just as no one is 100 percent good. We often quote the verses that remind us that everyone is a sinner, but we also need to remind ourselves that when God looked at His creation He said, "It is good." There's good in everyone. It was put there by a good God. Whatever that good thing is in a person, it is a good gift intended to be used for good in the world.

Even Delilah had some good in her. In fact, she did at least four things that were *very, very RIGHT.*

First, Delilah understood who she was, how she was created, and how God had gifted her with her womanhood. She understood the power of her own femininity.

Femininity is a wonderful gift that is given by God to every woman. She can use it for good or she can use it to destroy. She can develop her femininity, or she can ignore it and try to put it down. Delilah used her gift in a destructive, manipulative way, but she at least knew that she had the gift. She understood her own womanhood and how powerful and awesome a gift she had been given.

Second, Delilah talked with Samson and affirmed him. A woman doesn't have to be beautiful to have a man if she will only learn how to talk with him. Delilah didn't just talk *to* Samson — she had conversations *with* him. She communicated with him. She listened to him. She spoke to the wounded ego inside him.

Many men are womanizers because deep down inside, they are hurting. They have a pain that comes from a lack of being told they are loved unconditionally. They are searching for someone who will speak words of praise, love, and appreciation to the wounded man inside who has never heard those words spoken in gentleness and kindness.

Men have been given a warrior spirit, a fighting spirit. It's a part of a man's God-given nature to win battles. And when a man wins a battle, he needs to be affirmed, to be praised, to be told "attaboy." He needs to hear someone say to him, "You were super, wonderful, spectacular, awesome." He may just be flicking the remote control for the television set, but he needs to hear, "You didn't go through all the channels; you knew exactly which one you wanted and you hit that button. I like a man who's decisive!"

Men need compliments, even if they are about things that are minor. Men have egos that are easily bruised. That's why they do some very silly things just to get praise. A man will go out on a cold day without a warm coat, perhaps wearing only a little windbreaker, and his wife will ask him, "Honey, aren't you cold?"

"No, I'm not cold. Not cold at all."

"You ought to be, with only that windbreaker."

"No, no, I'm just fine. I'm doing all right."

"Oh, you're so strong."

And at that point, the man might be freezing to death but he won't admit it! His wife thinks he's strong! He may come down with a bad cold, but it felt so good to be told he was strong that he wouldn't dare admit he was chilled to the bone.

Delilah knew how to talk with Samson, and as part of her conversation, she knew how to praise him and build him up. She knew how to focus on his *strength*, not on his weakness. Every man needs that kind of affirmation. In all honesty, I don't believe a man can live out his destiny on the earth unless he has a woman in his life who knows how to affirm him.

When my wife discovered the power of her words to bring life to my soul, she began to use that ability to make me stand taller than I ever thought. I now can't wait to hear what she has to say about my messages, how I'm dressed, and how wonderfully I put a deal together. And she has a way of correcting me — but I feel like the whole thing was my idea!

Man's need for affirmation is a part of his creation. It is a part of his being made in the image of God. In Genesis 1:3, we find the very first thing God said, **Let there be light: and there was light.** God had created the angelic host to be creatures bathed in light. This host was created to bring glory to God. They generated praise and glory in which God enthroned Himself and in which He operated.

To a great extent, every man needs a "host" that will praise him, that will wrap him in affirmation so he can operate fully as a creative force on the earth. Everything rests on that foundation.

> **For a man indeed ought not to cover his head, forasmuch as he is the image and glory of God: but the woman is the glory of the man.**
>
> **For the man is not of the woman; but the woman of the man.**
>
> **Neither was the man created for the woman; but the woman for the man.**
>
> **1 Corinthians 11:7-9**

In the presence of her husband, a woman operates to bring glory to her man. So many men today aren't the men they could be because they do not have wives who are affirming them. Instead, they have wives who complain and pull them down and talk about nothing but their shortcomings. When a woman starts to build up her man and "call those things that are not as though they were," she builds him up and affirms him so he can operate in the fullness of who he is *supposed* to be in the Lord.

A woman is wise if she will look at the good traits God has put into her man and start to stroke, lift up, and praise those traits. The same goes for sons. They need to hear a mother's praise of their good qualities and affirmation for who God has made them to be.

Third, Delilah touched Samson. She was so warm toward Samson that he thought very little could happen to him when he told her his secret and then put his head on her lap.

Wife, when was the last time you really touched your husband? God made your hands soft, your skin pretty. He didn't pull you from the dirt. He pulled you from a place close to the heart with an ability to create warmth and to touch with gentleness and softness.

When you touch your husband with gentleness, he feels the other part of himself coming alive. He was pulled from the dirt — God made man from the dust. Man knows what it's like to face the elements and to be touched by pain, harsh conditions, and troubles. When he feels a woman's touch, he is reminded of that part of himself that was pulled out by God when He made woman. There's a healing and a wholeness that fills his being.

Nothing can calm the spirit of a man like the soft touch of a woman. When a man comes in from the cruelties of the day and his wife says to him as he walks through the front door, "Come on in. Lay down and let me just touch you for awhile," that man feels restored to his full identity. He feels at peace inside himself.

Samson wasn't satisfied with a prostitute. She touched him physically, but not with a sense of intimacy that touched his heart and his soul. She only gave him sex. Delilah gave him intimacy, and he loved her for it.

Fourth, Delilah gave Samson a place to rest. Samson was a man on the move. He went from one battle to the next. But when he went to Delilah, he was going to a place where he could rest, sleep, relax, unwind, be himself, express himself, and eventually share his deepest secrets about himself.

So many men get into wrong environments and wrong relationships because they have no place to rest their full identities. They are searching for a place to call "home" in their souls. They may even seek out a woman with whom to have an affair, because they don't have a place to "rest" themselves fully.

I didn't realize it when I was a child, but in looking back, I realize my mother gave my father a place to rest. All I knew then was that I was getting slammed into my bed at eight-thirty and told to go to sleep. That was about the time Daddy was coming home. When he got home, he walked into a house that was spotlessly clean. His dinner was waiting to be served. Mamma had made a place where my father could rest himself.

Now Daddy was not a gentle man. In many ways, he was a hard man. He could be rude and abrupt. But my mother chose to see in my father the man who would eventually build four churches, a man of great vision and energy. She saw that in my father long before it was a reality.

My father had a vision for the lives of his sons and he could be tough in his efforts to see that vision come to pass. After the seventh grade, he felt his obligation to me was fulfilled apart from putting a roof over my head and food on the table. He expected me to work for whatever else I wanted. At the time I hated him for that, but once I got out of the house as a young adult, I loved him for it, because I knew how to take care of myself. I was the first of any person in our family ever to graduate from college. I had a self-confidence by the time I left home that was born in part of my father's hardness.

My mother honored and respected the "visionary" that my father was. She gave him a place where he could rest himself in peace and quietness — a place where he could really be himself.

God can't speak to a man whose spirit is never at rest. Being at peace on the inside is necessary if a man is to hear what God wants to say, or to see what God wants to reveal. If a woman wants her husband to change, the first thing she should do is create an environment in which her husband's spirit can be at rest. God can then minister to him. If a woman tries to get her husband to change, but she doesn't create that environment first, she is only adding to his pain and pressure. He'll never hear God over the nagging of his wife.

To make things worse, if a man doesn't find rest at home, he'll go out seeking a place of rest. It may not be to a prostitute or to a lover — it may be to the local pool hall where he is affirmed and made to feel that he can be at peace. It may be to the house of a friend. It may be to stay late at the office, where others who are staying late make him feel like he's important.

When a man seeks rest apart from his wife, he's always open game for the devil. He might go to a friend's house and find himself thinking, "Look at how his wife serves us while we're watching the game. My wife won't even let me invite anyone over to our house. He's got a better deal." And the seeds of unfaithfulness are planted in that man's heart by the devil, who can hardly wait to bring someone along who will *look* as if she can provide a place of rest for him.

Or, he may go out with a friend and find himself relaxing with that friend when cocaine is brought into the room. His friend says, "Here's the best relief from stress I've ever found." In his search for peace, the temptation is going to be strong to use that drug to help him unwind and feel at rest.

Men crave rest. They crave affirmation and gentle touching. They crave the presence of a woman who knows she is a woman and who knows how to express her femininity. If a man doesn't have that craving fulfilled at home with his wife, he will seek out a Delilah — or something that functions like a Delilah in his life.

A CAUTION TO SINGLE WOMEN

If you are a single woman reading this today, I caution you: Don't ask God for a husband unless you're willing to take care of him. Wake up to the fact that there is great power in your womanhood, in your femininity. God's desire is that you use your womanhood to affirm a husband, to touch him with your gentleness, and to create a place where he can rest his soul. These are the things Delilah did *right*. They are the right things for every wife to do in loving her husband. And unless you are willing to do these things for a man, you are going to be much happier staying a single woman.

NEVER UNDERESTIMATE THE INFLUENCE OF A WIFE!

The story is told of a mayor of a prominent city who was on his way to a prestigious gathering one night. When he noticed that he was low on gas, he pulled into a gas station. As he and his wife sat in their fancy car, all dressed for the formal occasion, they noticed that the service station attendant was a man who had gone to school with him. In fact, the wife of the mayor had once dated him. The three of them had a casual conversation and then, since they were running late, the mayor and his wife hurried on.

As they drove away, the mayor — in all his prominence, pride, and self-importance — said,

"Honey, aren't you glad you married the mayor instead of marrying that gas station attendant?"

She replied, "No, not really."

He said, "What? Not really? What do you mean?"

She said, "Well, if I'd married him, you would be the gas station attendant and he would be the mayor."

This woman understood her power of influence. She understood, "Whoever I marry, whatever God has put in him, I'm going to make sure it comes out of him. I'm going to follow, I'm going to stroke him, encourage him, fill in the blanks of his life, help with the details, trust God to speak to him and deal with him, and over time, I'm going to help him become all that he can be in the Lord and in God's kingdom."

This woman hadn't nagged her husband into being mayor. She had *built him up* on the inside so he could *be* the mayor.

My wife is always trying to make me look good. She just does it naturally. One time she was trying to brush something off her lap and I thought it was a sign to me that I had something on me that I needed to get rid of — so I began looking around nervously for what was wrong. In the end, I found out she didn't mean anything by it. But she has so sensitized me to her every gesture, I'm always "looking!" I know ˙my wife desires for me to present my best image, and because she wants what is best for me, I want it too!

A warrior man can't be forced to change or become something he doesn't want to become. He can't be conned, coaxed, or coerced into it. But he can be *inspired* to be the best he can be in every way.

INFLUENCE BY QUIET EXAMPLE

When I first went to New Birth Church as its pastor, I was the polyester king. On certain Sundays, I perspired so much in my hot, no-breathing-room polyester suits that I could have welcomed in the flood. Then I got married.

Glory was created around me in the presence of my wife.

And you know, my wife never once talked to me about my polyester suits or about the perspiration problem they caused. Never! In fact, she never said anything at all about the way I dressed. Yet somehow, she was able to motivate me to dress better. I think it may have been that I could see how much she admired stylish dressing and I wanted to impress her. She never said a word, but before long, I was shopping for new suits.

It's in the power of every woman to take a bum and make a king out of him. God gave that creative ability to women. They have the capability to put an atmosphere of glory around their man — to affirm him, touch him, and give him a place of rest in the midst of their praise and affirmation and love. A man in that environment of glory is going to come to himself and be open to God, to grow, and to come into the fullness of who he is!

On the other hand, if a woman pushes her man, criticizes him, badgers him, nags him, and creates anything but "glory" around him, he's going to feel more pain and pressure. He'll be driven away to seek the glory he craves, the affirmation and gentle touching he needs, and the place where he can feel at home in his soul.

It's in the power of the woman to create a "place" for her man. And in creating the place, she establishes what her man can become in Christ.

THE HEALING
POWER OF A WOMAN

When a woman operates out of her inner beauty of character to influence her husband and children, to nurture them, and to influence them by her godly traits, she truly becomes an agent for healing and change on the earth. I truly do not believe that anything God wants to have happen on the earth is going to happen unless real women of God are fulfilling their role and are walking in the ways God has called them to walk. Isaiah 58:6-9 (NKJV) is for women today:

> **Is this not the fast that I have chosen: to loose the bonds of wickedness, to undo the heavy burdens, to let the oppressed go free, and that you break every yoke?**
>
> **Is it not to share your bread with the hungry, and that you bring to your house the poor who are cast out; when you see the naked, that you cover him, and not hide yourself from your own flesh?**

> **Then your light shall break forth like the morning, your healing shall spring forth speedily, and your righteousness shall go before you; the glory of the Lord shall be your rear guard.**

> **Then you shall call, and the Lord will answer; you shall cry, and He will say, "Here I am."**

Embrace your role as a godly woman! Choose to minister to others out of a great strength of godly character, but also with a softness that nurtures and enriches others. God has given you a wonderful role to play. Choose to walk in it!

HEADSHIP AND HELPMATES

When I marry a couple, I often use this analogy: I have two keys joined together by a ring, which symbolizes that the keys have been "married." One of the keys opens one lock on the door, and the other key opens another lock on the door. The keys are not interchangeable and both keys must be used for the door to open. That's the way it is in marriage. A man has a role to fill. A woman has a role to fill. And both roles must be filled for a marriage to be successfully established and sustained.

I have met countless women who have bought the devil's lie that they are to be "equal in function" to men and they are miserable in that lie. They have gone after something that has no potential to fulfill them as human beings.

Women most certainly are equal to men in spirit. Let there be no doubt about that. But God's plan is *not* that men and women function equally.

GOD'S PATTERN OF COVERING

From the beginning of creation, we see a pattern of "covering." God covered the spirit of man with flesh. He also covered the spirit of man with Himself. A woman was created to be covered spiritually by man. Man was pulled out of the earth physically. Woman was pulled out of man physically. In the spirit realm, God "begat" Adam, and he used Adam to "begat" Eve.

Isaiah 4:1 speaks of the covering that women have in men: **And in that day seven women shall take hold of one man, saying, We will eat our own bread, and wear our own apparel: only let us be called by thy name, to take away our reproach.** These women were saying, in effect, "We'll pay for our own food and buy our own clothes, but give us your name, because we need a man's covering." God made women to be covered by men both socially and spiritually.

Spiritually, a woman is under her father's covering until she leaves his home to be under her husband's cover. If there is an interim period between the father's covering and the husband's covering, she is under the spiritual covering of her pastor. The covering I am speaking of is a prayer covering. There is always this covering available to the woman.

As a mother, a woman is a covering for her child. God uses her to beget a child physically, and along with her husband, a mother provides a covering for her child. This covering is primarily an emotional covering.

I can vividly recall the day when my mother packed her bags to leave my father because he had been acting in a foolish way. I went to her and said,

"Mamma, if you leave, I'll die." She took one look at me, my eyes all swollen from crying, and she said, "I'm not going anywhere." She unpacked her bags and stayed.

My mother covered me emotionally with her presence, even when my father acted in error.

Covering Is Related to Completion. The important thing to understand about covering is that it is related to your sense of completion. If you are a man, you need to have something to cover in order for you to feel complete. If you are a woman, you need to be covered to feel complete. Children need their parents' covering to feel whole.

The creation of man was God's fulfillment of creation. For reasons known and understood only by God, God needed a man for His creation to be complete. Genesis 2:4-7 tells us about man's creation:

> These are the generations of the heavens and of the earth when they were created, in the day that the Lord God made the earth and the heavens,
>
> And every plant of the field before it was in the earth, and every herb of the field before it grew: for the Lord God had not caused it to rain upon the earth, and there was not a man to till the ground.
>
> But there went up a mist from the earth, and watered the whole face of the ground.
>
> And the Lord God formed man of the dust of the ground, and breathed into his nostrils the breath of life; and man became a living soul.

God wanted a man for His creation and He made a man. What God wants, God always gets. He formed the man from the dust of the earth and then breathed His own Spirit into him.

After He had made man, who began to function on the earth under God's authority, God looked and said, "It's not good for man to be alone, all by himself. I'm going to make him a helper." He caused Adam to go into a deep sleep, and he pulled from Adam a rib and used it to make a woman as Adam's helper. God saw that just as His creation had not been complete without a man for Him to cover with His presence, so Adam's creation was not complete without a woman to cover.

There are a few men whom God specifically calls to be single for the unique purposes God has for that man's life, but for the vast majority of men, God intends marriage. Men simply are not fulfilled in themselves unless they have a woman to cover, and a woman who in turn will be a helper to him. The vast majority of men will find they can never really be the full person or walk in the fullness of what God has ordained for them unless they have a godly woman by their side.

WHAT KIND OF HELPER DID GOD MAKE FOR MAN?

Eve was not created by God to help Adam "look good" as she took his arm and walked through the earth with him. Many men seem to think that the best help a woman can give him is to help him "look good" or "look macho" in the eyes of his friends.

Eve, however, was not brought to Adam on the basis of her good looks. God did not create Eve and then say to Adam, "Look at what a fine-looking woman I made for you. She's a real babe!"

The fact is, Adam wasn't even asking for a woman when God made Eve. He seemed quite happy to be playing with the tiger cubs and swinging through the trees with the orangutans and coming up with the right names for the elephant and the giraffe. It was God who said, **It is not good that the man should be alone; I will make him an help meet for him** (Genesis 2:18).

When God introduced Eve to Adam, He introduced her by her job description: helpmate. He had made for Adam a mate "suitable" to help him.

We must always keep in mind that God's definition of a "helpmeet" is not someone to raise the children, do the housekeeping, cook the meals, wash the dishes, or do the laundry. *God made Eve when none of those chores existed!* Even so, He said about Adam, "He needs a helper."

We must conclude, therefore, that being a helpmeet does *not* mean to be a slave in the house. Neither does it mean to have the primary responsibility for raising the children. A woman was not created with the expressed purpose to be merely a baby-sitter and housekeeper.

In actuality, the primary responsibility for children is the husband's, just as the primary spiritual responsibility for the family is the husband's. The primary responsibility for provision and protection for the family is the husband's.

Man has been given a tremendous task to do — not only in the spiritual realm, but in the physical, natural, and material realm — and he needs a "helper" if he is going to do it all to the glory of God.

So what kind of helper is it that God saw man needed?

The real help that a woman is to provide for a man lies in her ability to help him live a Christlike life by building him up emotionally and spiritually. One way a woman might help a man emotionally and spiritually may lie in her helping him with the details of his life — which may include fixing meals for him and keeping a nice home for him. But the real function of being a "helper" lies in the spiritual realm. A woman is to help a man live a godly life and to become everything he was created to be by God.

Many women today are frustrated because they find themselves in a position of being willing to help someone who isn't trying to do anything on his own! It's very discouraging for a woman to try to help a man who is sitting on a log or hanging out with other guys at the corner, happy *not* to be doing anything that just might require the help of another person.

Woman was created to help. Man was created with the need for help. Until a woman finds a person to help, and a man recognizes his need for help and avails himself of that help, neither a woman nor a man can be fulfilled in a marriage.

CONSEQUENCES OF THE FALL

What happened when Adam and Eve sinned and were expelled from the garden? A new order was imposed upon their lives by God.

The order God gave to the woman was this:

I will greatly multiply thy sorrow and thy conception; in sorrow thou shalt bring forth children; and thy desire shall be to thy husband, and he shall rule over thee.

Genesis 3:16

To the man, God said:

Because thou hast hearkened unto the voice of thy wife, and hast eaten of the tree, of which I commanded thee, saying, Thou shalt not eat of it: cursed is the ground for thy sake; in sorrow shalt thou eat of it all the days of thy life;

Thorns also and thistles shall it bring forth to thee; and thou shalt eat the herb of the field;

In the sweat of thy face shalt thou eat bread, till thou return unto the ground; for out of it wast thou taken: for dust thou art, and unto dust shalt thou return.

Genesis 3:17-19

Now why did God establish these new orders for Adam and Eve? In part because of what God had said to the serpent:

Because thou hast done this, thou art cursed above all cattle, and above every beast of the field; upon thy belly shalt thou go, and dust shalt thou eat all the days of thy life.

Genesis 3:14

We must see the connection here or we will miss the truth of how God wants us to relate as husbands and wives, and as fathers and mothers. The devil had been cast out of heaven and fell to the earth — no more to fly like the winged angelic being that he was, but to crawl upon the dust of the earth. Adam and Eve were expelled into a world in which the devil was going to be present with them always.

Furthermore, the devil was going to continue to come after Adam and Eve with the intent of destroying the "seed" of the woman — the offspring, the children, the future generations. The devil's number one intent is always to put a stop to the next generation, because if he can ever put a complete stop to a generation, he'll have put an end to the ongoing glory of God on the earth.

If Adam and Eve were to survive in this new reality, Eve was going to have to continue to desire her husband so she would bear children, even though the process was painful for her. And Adam would have to continue to struggle to provide for his wife and their children through the harsh reality of work, even though that process was painful for him. It was his responsibility to ensure that his children survive and reach maturity so the next generation after theirs could be birthed.

Adam must continue to cover Eve and their children, and Eve must bear children if they were to have any hope for their lives. The apostle Paul spoke of this to Timothy when he said,

> **Notwithstanding she shall be saved in child-bearing, if they continue in faith and charity and holiness with sobriety.**
>
> **1 Timothy 2:15**

Paul did not mean that a woman is saved spiritually by having a baby. He meant that a woman's purpose was completed, enacted, or fulfilled in a family's battle with the devil when she bore a child and reared that child in the nurture and admonition of the Lord, because her child moved Christianity forward into the next generation. Even if a woman doesn't bear a child out of her natural womb, she has the potential to "birth" children spiritually, bringing the lost to a new birth experience in Christ. In a real and wonderful way, she moves Christianity forward to the next generation through this birthing of spiritual children.

The good news lies in what God said in Genesis 3:15 — **I will put enmity between thee and the woman, and between thy seed and her seed; it shall bruise thy head, and thou shalt bruise his heel.**

Even in the curses God gave to the devil, woman, and man, He had a plan for the total redemption of men and women. The seed of the woman would bring about a defeat of the devil! That seed, of course, was manifested in Jesus. He won the victory over the devil.

Even so, the battle still rages. The victory is won, but not yet consummated. A turning point has occurred and the end result is assured, but we still must fight on to the end in the "mop-up" battles. We are beloved and betrothed to Christ, but we are not yet His bride in heaven. The devil is still bound to this earth. Therefore, our warfare against him must continue.

As part of our fight against Satan, we are to bear and raise up children — both physically and spiritually. For that to happen, a woman is going to have to continue to desire her husband and seek to bear children. A man is going to have to continue to provide for his wife and children and raise them to maturity.

Never, never, never lose sight of the fact that God's ultimate plan is for redemption — not only the redemption of Adam and Eve, but the redemption of every person who has ever lived. If we are going to defeat the devil and live truly victorious lives, we must first come to an acceptance of Jesus Christ as our Savior, follow Him in obedience, and live out God's plan for the defeat of the devil — women desiring their husbands and bearing children, men working hard all of their lives to protect and provide for their wives and children. The family is God's plan for defeating the devil — it is His vehicle, His design.

GOD'S CHAIN OF COMMAND

God installed a pattern of covering in His initial creation that made the relationship between man and woman complete. Likewise, when He instituted a new order after the fall, He initiated a pattern that might be called "a chain of command" in order that the relationship between man and woman might work.

Covering is related to completion. Chain of command is related to functional, operational "working." This chain of command runs throughout God's creation.

The fact is, *everyone* is under the authority of a "higher power" of some type. The head of Christ is God the Father. Jesus said very plainly that He didn't do anything of His own authority, but only what He saw the Father doing. (See John 5:19.)

Every man is under the authority of either Jesus Christ or under the influence of the devil; a Christian man certainly is under the authority of Christ. The head of woman is man — her father until she is married, her husband after her marriage, and if there is an interim period, her pastor. Children are under the authority of their parents.

The One Who Is Responsible Has Authority. Very clearly throughout God's Word, the chain of command functions according to this principle: The person who has authority has responsibility, and the person who has been given the responsibility has the authority.

There's nothing worse than being in a position in which you have been given responsibility for getting a job done, but you have been given no authority to do it. God's plan is clear: If you have the responsibility for something, you have the authority to act.

When I first came to my church as pastor, I was given all the responsibility that comes with that position, but the authority rested in the hands of the church boards. Needless to say, I was not able to function as God ordained because my authority was usurped. Slowly, through teaching on the biblical chain of command in the church, the boards submitted themselves to scriptural authority, which gave me the authority that was rightfully mine to do what God charged me to do.

If a man is responsible for the protection and provision of his wife and children, he has the authority over them. If a woman is to be responsible for the protection and provision of her children, she has authority over them. In like manner, since Jesus Christ is responsible for the protection and provision of the Church, He has authority over it.

When it comes to the rest of creation, God has authority over all of creation, but He has given man dominion over a portion of His creation — the portion related to animals, fish, and birds. Mankind has responsibility for other creatures and authority over them. Everyone and everything operates according to the chain of command, to an order of responsibility and authority.

There are three key concepts that are directly related to authority and they are at the foundation of the way a husband and wife are to relate:

- Respect

- Submission

- Obedience

In each case, those who are lower on the chain of command are told to respect, submit, and obey those who are above them on the chain of command. In a marriage relationship, a husband is to respect, submit to, and obey God. A wife is to respect, submit to, and obey her husband. Children are to respect, submit to, and obey their parents.

Paul wrote to the Ephesians, **Let every one of you in particular so love his wife even as himself; and the wife see that she reverence her husband** (Ephesians 5:33).

This word "reverence" does not mean to worship spiritually. It means to *respect one's position within the chain of command.* Most of us can sing a little of that old Aretha Franklin song: R-E-S-P-E-C-T. Respect is what God expects wives to show to their husbands.

Of the three principles related to authority and responsibility — respect, submission, and obedience — respect is the one that has a two-way flow. Wives are not the only party in a marriage relationship who are responsible for showing respect. Husbands are also to be respectful of their wives. Respect is saying to one another, "I acknowledge and honor the fact that God has created you with a specific role and function. I also acknowledge that you are my equal in spiritual essence."

Equal in spiritual essence.

Different in practical function.

That is the pattern ordained by God for men and women in marriage. Respect is rooted in acknowledging that pattern and submitting to that pattern before God.

Position, Not Person. When you respect another person, you are acknowledging that person's "position" before God. Respect is not intended to be based upon what a person says or does, but rather, respect is for the position the person occupies before God. You may dislike some of the behaviors or even some of the personality characteristics of your spouse, but you are still called to respect the person's position before God — not only their position within the marriage, but their very creation as a beloved human being with a divine call and purpose for their life.

How can you respect the position of a person without respecting all of the behaviors of a person? It requires faith.

Faith. A principal ingredient of respect is faith. It takes faith for a wife to respect her husband, or for a husband to respect his wife. Respect is founded on the belief that God is in control of our lives, that He placed you with your current spouse, and that He is doing a work not only in your spouse through your life and position in the marriage, but in *you* through your spouse's life and position in the marriage. The trust is to be placed in God and in what God is seeking to accomplish in both of you, as well as to accomplish in the lives of your children and others who are watching the witness of your family.

Psalm 127:1 tells us, **Except the Lord build the house, they labour in vain that build it.** You can't truly respect your spouse unless your faith is in God. It is out of your faith and trust in God that respect for your spouse will flow.

So many people are rising up early, going to bed late, and eating the bread of sorrow all the day long because they are trying to live their lives on their own ability, talent, and energy. It can't be done! The same principle applies to marriage. You can't "work up" respect for your spouse on your own. It is something that comes from God as you place your faith solely in Him for the success of your marriage.

Competition. One of the things we must defeat in the Church is the spirit of Jezebel. I'm not just talking about Ahab's wife. I'm referring to the man-hating, get-what-you-want spirit that Jezebel embodied. Jezebel had no respect for her husband. She was in strong competition with him for the ultimate authority over the land. She was out to mold Ahab into what *she* thought a king should be, not what God thought Ahab should be as king. There are many women today who have this spirit toward men in general, and toward their husband in particular. A competitive spirit and respect simply do not mix.

Let me speak directly to the women — God has made your man the way He made him, and God is capable of correcting him and leading him. It is not up to you to fashion and design your husband into the person *you* want him to be. The more you try to do that, the more your husband will rebel and the more frustrated you are going to be.

What has God ordained men to be?

Steadfast.

Immovable.

Always abounding.

Determined that whatever God wants done *will* be done.

Your husband may counsel with you and ask for and listen to your opinion. He may yield to your suggestions. He may very well give you the things you express you need or desire. But when a husband has finally made up his mind about a direction to move or an action to take, he is going to do what he has determined to do. No nagging will dissuade him. And he will not tolerate disrespect. He'll move on to someone who will respect him.

SUBMISSION

Just as respect relates to position, submission relates to decision-making. Submission is not limited to husband-wife relationships, as so many seem to think. It is a concept related to all of the "chain of command" within the Church. In Ephesians 5:21 Paul says that believers should be **submitting yourselves one to another in the fear of God.** This is the statement he makes just before he says, **Wives, submit yourselves unto your own husbands, as unto the Lord** (Ephesians 5:22).

As Christians we are to submit to one another so we can come to a position of having one mind in Christ Jesus — of being in agreement in prayer and the Spirit. This kind of unity is advocated throughout the New Testament where we find many references to having one Lord, one baptism, one faith, one Spirit, one calling, one hope. (See Ephesians 4:1-6.) So submission becomes a major issue any time a decision is made.

When a husband and wife are facing a decision, there should be a discussion. The couple should talk things through, each bringing to the discussion his and her unique understanding of the matter. A woman brings to the discussion her best intuitive and emotional sensitivity. A man brings to the discussion his best reason, rationality, and objectivity. They talk things through.

The decision rests with the one who has both responsibility and authority. A man who truly is operating in a reasonable and rational way will certainly weigh the arguments made by his wife and consider the insights she has. She may be absolutely accurate and correct in the matter! He needs her insight because he can't think like she can.

Then the husband must make a decision. He has the responsibility for that decision, therefore he has the authority for that decision. The decision must be made and communicated with love, not as a tyrannical dictator. He should be able to give his reasons for his decision. And once he has made a decision, that decision must stand until he makes a different decision, alters his decision, or another problem arises which requires an amended decision.

In this area of submission the apostle Peter noted that Sarah called Abraham "lord." Peter advised women that since they are daughters of Sarah, they should also call their husbands "lord." (See 1 Peter 3:6.) This does not mean that a woman should worship her husband rather than Jesus Christ, or even in the same manner as Jesus Christ. Jesus is Lord of lords, King of kings. Neither does it mean that she should call him lord rather than by his name. It means that in her heart, she must submit to her husband as a queen submits to her king.

In the natural, physical, and material world in which a wife lives with her husband, she must acknowledge her husband as the king of the house and the lord of the manor. She must respect his position of headship in the home. This yielding to headship is the basis on which a woman leaves her father's house and name and takes the name of her husband. Before my wife married, she was Vanessa Griffin because her father's name was Griffin. She's now Vanessa Long. She has come under my headship, my covering.

No woman can have two heads. Two-headed beasts are freaks. When a woman marries, she needs to take her husband's name and place her identification under his covering. If she isn't willing to accept the name of the one who is assuming the responsibility and authority for protecting her and providing for her, she shouldn't marry.

A WOMAN DOESN'T LOSE ANYTHING BY SUBMITTING

This is a very important point: Position in the chain of authority has nothing to do with the individual's worth to God or the person's value to others. Each of us is supremely valuable to God and to His plan.

No Loss of Spiritual Power. A woman who is subject to her husband can go directly to God in prayer just as her husband does. She can request what she wants and receive her answer from God just as quickly and just as directly as a man. A woman's prayers are answered just as readily as a man's. The gifts of the Spirit flow through a woman just as they do through a man. Joel 2:28 foretold the day in which we live: **I will pour out my spirit upon all flesh; and your sons and your daughters shall prophesy.**

The only time a woman loses her spiritual power is when she disobeys the Word of God or the Spirit of God — just the same as a man. Her husband is not going to get his prayers answered if he is abusing her or treating her badly. In the same way, if a woman defies God's chain of command and does not respect her husband, nagging, complaining, and putting him down all the time, she's not going to see her prayers answered either.

A woman is called to obey the commandments of God just as man must obey. She is called to read and understand the Word of God for herself. She is called to pray and to intercede for others just as a man is. She is called to be in fellowship with other Christians and to serve in the Church just as a man is. Before God, a woman is equal in spiritual essence.

Spiritual equality means that a woman can preach, teach, prophesy, and operate in all of the gifts of the Spirit. She can give a witness to Jesus Christ. Whatever is made possible by the Holy Spirit, a woman can do! A woman doesn't just receive a "part" of God's Holy Spirit when she is born again. She receives the Holy Spirit in fullness. She has both the capacity and the privilege of expressing the Holy Spirit fully in her ministry to others.

No Loss of Talents. Just as a person doesn't lose anything spiritually in marriage, neither does a person lose creative ability or personal gifts and talents. A woman has just as much ability to produce, create, design, and show her individual flair and style to the world. There is no loss of intelligence or capability to think, plan, and function. A woman has just as much worth and is just as important after marriage as she was before marriage.

No Loss of Value. A woman is not inferior to man. Many men and some women with very low self-esteem have bought a lie from the devil that women are inferior to men. They base this on the fact that women aren't as strong physically, aren't as rational overall in their thinking, and aren't as competitive.

Peter tells us that a woman is a "weaker vessel," but at no time does he say that a woman is an inferior vessel. Rather than look down on a woman because she is weaker, Peter tells husbands to give honor to their wives. (See 1 Peter 3:7.) There is no justification in God's Word for a man to "put down" a woman as having less value than a man.

No Less Free in Her Spirit. Submission has nothing to do with the freedom a woman is to feel in her spirit. When Peter writes to the wives **likewise, ye wives,** we must take into account the broader context in which he is writing. In the verses just prior to these verses on respect and submission,

Peter tells *all* in the church, both men and women, that God requires orderly obedience to all of the laws and regulations of the land. He tells slaves to submit to their masters. And he teaches that freedom does not lie in outward behavior or relationships, but in the inner spirit of a person.

A wife's obedience, submission, and respect to her husband should not result in her feeling less "free" on the inside — either emotionally or spiritually. Her real freedom can only be provided by Christ Jesus anyway. There are women who are single and totally free from submitting to a husband who aren't "free" in their spirits. Freedom is not related to your marital state or outer condition. It is related to your spiritual relationship with the Lord.

A wife is not free to do what she likes in her behavior, but neither is a man. He is under authority to Christ. He very likely is also under the authority of his boss or supervisor at work. Freedom doesn't exist because he's the husband. Freedom is a matter of who he is on the inside in relation to Jesus Christ.

SUBMISSION IS AN ACT OF FAITH

Just as respect is an act rooted in faith, so is submission. There's no guarantee to the woman that her husband is going to make the right decision! In fact, he may very well make a wrong decision. Nevertheless, he must be obeyed. The woman's faith must not rest in the man's decision to be right, but rather, that God can work all things to His good — even a bad decision. Romans 8:28 is the verse to cling to:

And we know that all things work together for good to them that love God, to them who are the called according to his purpose.

When you want God's best and are believing for God's best, you can trust God to work, even if a husband errs. God never asks us to wait until it's "safe" to submit. He didn't ask Joshua to wait until the water parted before the priests stepped into the riverbed with the ark of the covenant. No — they were called to step into the river first and *then* the waters parted.

Faith means moving forward and acting in obedience to God's plan even if you suspect the one you are obeying is mistaken. God will honor your obedience, your submission, and your faith. *He will not honor your rebellion, even if you are "right" in your thinking.*

It is by submitting to your husband, even when he errs, that he gains confidence that you are supporting him and desiring his best. A wife's submission to her husband puts him into an even greater sense of responsibility to do the right thing before God.

Now I'm not talking about going out drinking with him, prostituting yourself for him, or delivering drugs for him. Your first loyalty is always to God and His Word. But you can *respectfully* and *submissively* refuse to *obey* your husband when he is going against God. Respect and submission are *attitudes,* but obedience is an *action.* You can have the right attitude toward your husband while you obey God and not him. You can say, "Honey, I love you and you're my man. But if I help you into sin I will be helping to bring you down. I love you too much to do that." In most disagreements, however, the issues are not so extreme. The husband just wants to spend money in a way the wife thinks is a waste or go in a direction she believes will lead nowhere.

Many women today are waiting for their husbands to get right with God and start doing all the right things before they submit. The exact opposite is required. When they submit to their husbands, their husbands are going to have a new desire to get right with God and start doing the right things!

> **Likewise, ye wives, be in subjection to your own husbands; that, if any obey not the word, they also may without the word be won by the conversation of the wives;**
>
> **While they behold your chaste conversation coupled with fear.**
>
> **1 Peter 3:1,2**

Peter advises women that even if their husbands aren't saved or don't have a solid knowledge of God's Word, they still must be in submission to their husbands. And the good news is that God will honor their submission and cause their husbands to be influenced by the God-honoring way they talk and act toward their husbands.

I know a number of married women whose husbands aren't saved and they routinely go out on Saturday morning with evangelistic teams to witness to people about Christ or to minister to others in Christ's name. The biggest problem with their ministry is that they are aiming it in the wrong direction. They need to stay home and do some ministry to their husbands!

I've had other women come to me complaining that their ungodly husbands have no interest in God — in fact, the only thing they seem to be interested in is sex. Well, if that man is the woman's husband, and what he's interested in is sex, it is in sex that she needs to minister to her husband. It's a legal ministry! When she ministers to him in that way, he's going to feel built up on the inside. Something emotional is going to be healed in him to the point where he *can* hear the Gospel.

No woman can force a man to give up his sinful self and become what God ordained him to be. And a woman certainly can't influence a man to become more spiritual if she is neglecting the emotional and physical needs of her husband!

Submission is more important than "being right." You are probably thinking, *Are you saying that even if I'm right and I know my husband is wrong, I should submit to his decision?* Yes. Discuss his decision with him to the best of your ability, but then once the decision is made by him, submit to it. As you do, trust

God to correct the error, right the wrong, fix the situation, and take care of you in the midst.

Were the Roman rulers in error when they allowed Christ Jesus to be crucified? Of course. Even Pilate admitted that Jesus had done nothing to warrant punishment by death.

Were the Jewish rulers of the Temple in error when they insisted that Jesus be killed? Of course. He had done nothing to break the Law of Moses.

But did Jesus submit to the death of the cross? Absolutely. And He did so trusting God to work a greater good even though others were in error. He said from the cross, "Forgive them, for they don't know what they are doing."

Jesus willingly yielded His life. It wasn't taken from Him. He *submitted* His life to God and to death on the cross. He trusted God with the outcome — which truly was a great one. Not only did the outcome include Jesus' resurrection from the dead, but the way of salvation for countless millions upon millions of people. It was the definitive victory over the devil that will culminate in the final victory of the ages.

SUBMISSION HELPS A MAN TO SEE HIMSELF AND JESUS

When a husband looks at his wife, he should see in her an image of who he is supposed to be in Christ. In other words, he should see Jesus in his wife, and therefore see a character sketch of who he should be in Christ. A woman who lives like Jesus doesn't have to preach a word to her husband. Her very life and character are all the sermon she needs to give.

I've seen countless examples of a man being led to Christ by his wife's submissive, respectful, obedient behavior. In each case, these men saw in their wives a "higher image" of what it means to be a human being. They saw a Christlikeness that was attractive and desirable. And when a man decides he wants something, he goes after it. He moves toward Christ when Christ becomes appealing to him.

I had a woman complain to me one day that her husband never took out the trash. I told her that the next time trash day came around she should ask her husband to help *her* carry out the trash. I said, "Then, when he happens to be emptying that trash into the bin, you say to him, 'Hold it. I just saw something jump up in the back of your arm. What was that?' He'll have to admit it was a muscle. You applaud that muscle, saying, 'Well, lift that entire trash can up and let me see how good God is!' You tell him when you get in bed that night that you have a new appreciation for his strength. Trust me, if you praise his strength every time you need to take out the trash, he'll soon be saying, 'Hey, watch me. I'm about to take out the trash!'"

She took my advice, and she has never had to nag her husband again! He doesn't feel demeaned by having to take out the trash — he feels proud and strong in taking it out! In fact, he proudly says to his friends when they call, "I was out emptying the trash. You know, that really turns my wife on. It's gonna be fun at my house tonight!"

Before long, that man had a desire not only to be strong physically, but to become strong spiritually. He wasn't just taking out the heavy trash can from the house, he started emptying the trash from his soul, from his life.

In all seriousness, there's a *way* for a woman to build up her man in every area of their marriage — not so she can manipulate him, but to give him a desirable picture of what it means to be a strong, pure, and godly person in Christ Jesus.

MY MOTHER'S WITNESS TO MY FATHER

My mother discovered two major things about my father *after* she married him. She discovered the secret that he was an alcoholic, and she discovered he wasn't really saved. Yet because she married him and she knew the Scriptures, she submitted to my father and she respected him.

She got up early every morning and made breakfast from scratch for my daddy. And when my daddy came home — even when he came home late with some shaky excuse for being late — she would get out of bed and fix him a plate of food and sit with him until he finished it, wash the dishes, and have his clothes ready for the next day.

This wasn't fun for her. It wasn't the greatest life. There were lots of times when my father was a miserable person to be around. But if it hadn't been for this submissive spirit in my mother, I wouldn't be who or where I am today.

On Sunday mornings, my mother would make sure my father had all the "ministry" he needed before she got out of bed. If you are a woman today who says your husband won't let you go to church, I suggest you minister to him *first* and then get up and get ready for church.

My mother would get up, cook breakfast for my father and have it all ready for him — even if he didn't get up right away and eat it. And *then* she got ready for church. She told me one time, "Honey, when I would get ready to go to church, I'd make sure that I put on my stockings and my best dress and perfume all where he could watch me if he cared to take a peep. And then I'd walk out looking and smelling my best.

"After I did this for about a year, I noticed that he was watching me more and more. By the end of two years, he was sitting on the side of the bed watching me get ready for church. I walked by the outside window on my way to church with my very best "walk" — the one he loved to watch.

"And after about three and a half years of this, he got up one morning and when I looked around after getting ready for church, I found that he was dressed. He grabbed me by the arm and said, 'I'm going with you.'

"On that Sunday morning, the preacher gave a mighty sermon and your daddy got up, crossed over me, and walked down the aisle. Not only did he get saved that morning, but he felt God calling him into the ministry."

Not only did my father become a minister, but he founded many churches.

Who led my father to Christ? My mother. And how did she do it? Through respectful submission to him even when he was an unsaved alcoholic.

WORD OF CAUTION
TO SINGLE WOMEN

The moment you say "I do" and kiss, you start submitting in respect and obedience to your husband. If you don't want to be submitted, hold that kiss and don't make that vow. If you don't expect to abide under the rules of the covering that a husband offers a wife, don't get under the covering!

If you don't want to be submissive to a husband — respectful and obedient in teaching — don't get married. Don't let anyone push you into it because someone wants a grandchild, or someone thinks that a woman should be married by the time she's thirty, or because someone is accusing you of being a lesbian if you don't want to get married.

God calls some people to be single. And it's far better for a woman who doesn't desire to be a genuine helpmeet to a man to be single than to get into a marriage and try to function in that marriage in a manner that is apart from God's plan. She'll only be miserable in her attempt, never successful, and the man will be miserable too. In the end, the marriage will be a miserable state and if they conceive children, those children are not only going to be miserable, but they are going to have precisely the wrong role model to follow as they enter their own adult and childbearing years.

There's nothing unspiritual or unrighteous about being single. Paul was very clear on this. He pointed out that those who are single have more time to serve the Lord. (See 1 Corinthians 7:32-35.) But if you *do* desire to be married, then you must be willing to enter into a marriage according to the "rules" God has established for marriage if you want your marriage to be a good one for you, your husband, and your children.

OBEDIENCE BRINGS WISDOM

Just as respect is related to position and submission is related to decision-making, so obedience is related to "learning." Women are to be obedient in the sense that they are to receive and yield to a man's understanding. As we discussed earlier, men have a great ability to see the "big picture." They are rational creatures. Women have a great ability to see and to act upon details. They are more intuitive, emotional creatures. Both are important, but when it comes to an understanding of the whole truth, emotion must obey reason.

In 1 Timothy 2:11-14 we read this admonition:

Let the woman learn in silence with all subjection.

But I suffer not a woman to teach, nor to usurp authority over the man, but to be in silence.

For Adam was first formed, then Eve.

And Adam was not deceived, but the woman being deceived was in the transgression.

Learning in "silence with all subjection" means to be obedient in learning. The purpose for this learning is so that a woman will not be deceived.

Paul is referring back to Adam and Eve in this passage of his letter to Timothy. He notes that Eve was the one who talked to Satan, saw the tree, saw it was good for food and pleasant to the eye. She was the one who desired to eat to make herself wise. She took of the fruit first, ate it, then gave to her husband. She was deceived. Adam was not. Adam *knew* the consequences of eating the forbidden fruit. He was disobedient, but he was not deceived.

Many people today are of the opinion that women are more spiritually minded because they have a greater sensibility to spiritual things. It is true that women have a greater intuitiveness and that they are experts in "emotional thinking." This type of thinking is a gift from God and it is to be highly valued. It is needed for a balance to those who think only with cold objectivity and rationality. A woman's ability to think this way — intuitively, emotionally — does not necessarily mean, however, that she is more spiritually minded or that she is more correct on spiritual matters. This same spiritual sensitivity can result in spiritual error and the promotion of false doctrines.

It is for this reason that a woman needs the balance of a man's objectivity and knowledge of God's Word. She needs to place what she is thinking and feeling intuitively and emotionally before a person who is thinking objectively and from the standpoint of reason. When God spoke to man through Isaiah he said, **Come now, and let us reason together** (Isaiah 1:18). Men think in terms of what is reasonable, accurate, consequential, and factual. Intuition and emotional thinking always need to be subjected to this reason if the truth is to be established.

In his second letter to Timothy, the apostle Paul warns of false teachers who **creep into houses, and lead captive silly women laden with sins, led away with divers lusts, ever learning, and never able to come to the knowledge of the truth** (2 Timothy 3:6-7). These women to whom Paul refers are "learning," but they are learning because they are driven to learn by their lust. Now lust isn't limited to sexual behavior. It refers to a spirit of "wanting," of striving to get, get, get. Lust is rooted in a woman not having something she wants to have. These women are lusting to become like God just as Eve did. Because this is their motivation, Paul calls them "silly women" who are operating in a sinful manner. They never come to a knowledge of the truth because their motivation for learning

God's Word is wrong. A woman can never learn enough about God to *be* like God. Neither can a man, for that matter. Our learning is so we can follow God and be obedient to God, not so we can function *as* God.

Any time a person seeks to become more spiritual so they might have greater power over people or things, that person is "lusting" to be God. Our desire for spiritual power must always be a desire to learn how to trust God to defeat the devil as he attacks our lives and the lives of our loved ones, not so we can have more power over other people's lives.

Just about every type of spiritual teaching and spiritual guru is available to people today, and especially to women. Many of them are on radio and television programs that appeal primarily to women. A woman can easily be led to follow this preacher or that preacher and in her search for spirituality be led right down the primrose path to hell.

Let me give you an example of this type of intuitive, emotional thinking in the Bible. Sarah, the wife of Abraham, determined that she was past childbearing age. Abraham was supposed to father a child. Therefore, quite apart from God's commands and promises to her husband, she intuitively concluded that Abraham should father a child through her servant Hagar, and the two of them should raise that child as their own.

Sarah became impatient and unbelieving. This was *not* what God had commanded Abraham to do. It was what Sarah thought was a "good idea." Unfortunately, Abraham listened to Sarah and Ishmael was conceived. The result has been thousands of years of conflict between the Jews and the Arabs.

Sarah was playing God! She was way ahead of God's timing and totally out of line with God's method.

THE HUSBAND'S ROLE

One might conclude from this discussion of respect, submission, and obedience that men have a better deal. Such a conclusion is false. The same commands related to respect, submission, and obedience work in a man's life as he relates to Christ. In all cases:

• Respect is related to position.

• Submission is related to decision-making.

• Obedience is related to one's understanding of the whole truth of God on any given subject.

In addition, man has been given certain commands about how he is to relate to his wife.

Men are to exercise their headship with understanding. Peter wrote in his first epistle that men are to dwell with their wives "according to knowledge" and with honor...so their prayers will not be hindered. In the *New American Standard*

Bible, the verse is translated this way: **live with your wives in an understanding way, as with a weaker vessel, since she is a woman; and grant her honor as a fellow heir of the grace of life, so that your prayers may not be hindered** (1 Peter 3:7).

Most men I know believe that women are impossible to understand. But the Bible says that if our prayers are to be answered, a man must learn to live with his wife in an understanding way. To say that a woman can't be understood is a cop-out. That's an excuse for failing to take responsibility for gaining understanding.

The man who chooses not to study his wife and to gain understanding of his wife will eventually manifest the Adam syndrome — he will start blaming his wife for the problems in the marriage and beyond that, for his own problems. He'll say, as Adam did, "The woman *You* gave me, God, is the problem." (See Genesis 3:12.)

God didn't accept that excuse from Adam and He won't accept it from you either! There are no excuses for failing to gain an understanding of your wife.

A husband also must avoid a "vending machine mentality." Many men seem to have a vending-machine mentality when it comes to their marriages. They feel that there's something wrong with the "machine" if they don't get something out of it for all they think they're putting in.

A wife may complain, "You don't care about me."

The man's response is, "I'm putting a roof over your head, clothes on your back, and I've given you a car to drive and credit cards to use. What more do you want?" Everything about his tone and opinion says, "You've really got nerve. You ought to be grateful for all the care I do give you."

Believe me, a man *really* doesn't understand it when he gives everything he has of a material nature and works hard to provide for a woman and then she withholds sex from him. He begins to ask himself, "Why am I trying so hard when I'm not getting any appreciation or show of affection in return?"

The problem is, the husband doesn't understand what his wife is saying when she says, "You don't care about me." He hasn't gained an understanding that what she wants is an expression of value and affection and respect from him. She doesn't want *things*. She wants his praise, his approval, his recognition of her work and her effort.

What do men do when the vending machine doesn't give them the item they want after they put in their money? A good many of them kick or hit the machine — either to get the goods or to get their money back. There is never a good reason or excuse for abuse, but we must recognize that abuse is often triggered when a man does not feel that what he has done is sufficient. Men become abusers because they feel they are being put down or shut out, perhaps not by the person they abuse but by someone who isn't even in the room when the abuse occurs!

Jesus Christ calls a man to a different standard. Marriage is not a vending machine. A wife is not a vending machine. She is a valued treasure to be *understood*.

The more you understand a person — their backgrounds, their motivations, the way they communicate, their desires and dreams — the more compassion you feel for them, and generally speaking, the more mercy you show to them. Love wells up in you and your love begins to "cover" a multitude of sins and shortcomings.

When a husband begins to live with his wife in understanding of her, getting a true picture of how she is made and what she is capable of doing and being, he becomes more compassionate toward her. He extends mercy and forgiveness to her, just as Jesus *understands* our human frailties and continues to extend mercy and forgiveness to us.

But before a man can understand his wife and live in understanding with her, he must die to his own pride and get beyond himself and his selfish needs. He must extend himself to his wife just as Jesus Christ offered Himself to the world. As John said, **We love him, because he first loved us** (1 John 4:19).

Men who continue to say, "My wife is the problem," are men who haven't died to self and gained an understanding of their wives.

As far as I am concerned, the object of premarital counseling should always be to "gain understanding" about one another and to gain understanding about God's plan for marriage. When you marry a person, you aren't just marrying who that person is today. You are marrying years of personal history and even more years — yes, even generations — of family history. You may not know it at the time you marry, but you are marrying traits that exist in your spouse's parents, grandparents, and great-grandparents. Those things are going to come out in marriage. You need to have an understanding of them.

To gain an understanding requires a willingness to communicate — to open up and be transparent, to pray together — that you may begin to know each other's heart before God. This takes great courage, because it is out of this understanding that we come to a point of recognizing our weaknesses. Once we have recognized our weaknesses and faults, we are in a position to come to God and confess them, be forgiven for our sins, and to be healed of our "mess" — our bad memories, our mistakes, our errors, our flaws.

When husbands seek to understand their wives and love them and pray with them about each of their "messes," the "messes" get defeated, the husband and wife grow more mature in the Lord and more in love with Him and each other — and the marriage gets better and better.

THE JESUS FACTOR

Many a man errs in thinking he has a privilege to boss his wife, with a disregard of her needs and a total focus on getting his own needs met. He may be the king of his house, but Jesus Christ is King of kings. The ultimate throne is His. If he disregards his wife's needs, he can't expect the King of kings to give him what he needs. If he is totally self-centered, he leaves no room for Jesus to be honored as Lord of all.

If you do not extend mercy to your wife, how can you ask God for mercy?

If you do not honor your wife, even though she may be weaker physically, how can you ask God to honor you, who are weaker in comparison to Jesus Christ?

If you do not forgive, how can you receive forgiveness?

If you judge, how can you avoid being judged?

Jesus said very plainly,

> **Be ye therefore merciful, as your Father also is merciful.**
>
> **Judge not, and ye shall not be judged: condemn not, and ye shall not be condemned: forgive, and ye shall be forgiven:**
>
> **Give, and it shall be given unto you.**
>
> **Luke 6:36-38**

It's on this basis that Peter says, "Treat your wife right if you want your prayers to be heard and answered." (See 1 Peter 3:7.)

Jesus is to be our role model always. Study what He did. How did He relate to other people? What did He do with His time, His energy, His resources? How did He respond to the needs of "weaker" people?

If you as a husband want to know how to relate to your wife, study how Jesus related to His followers. What did He do for them? How did He respond to them? What kind of communication did He have with them? How did He show His love for them? Likewise, if you as a wife want to know how to relate to your husband, study how Jesus' followers related to Him. How did they submit to Him and what was His response?

When a woman knows that her husband is truly trying to understand her, that he values her, honors her, and considers her to be an "heir" with him of the grace of life, she rarely has a problem submitting to him. I have often said, "The better the husband, the better the wife. The better the father, the better the child."

If you truly want your marriage to improve, you can't start with the excuse or moaning, "If my wife would only..." To improve your marriage, you must start with yourself as the husband. If you truly want your family to improve, you can't say, "If only my kids would..." You must start with yourself as the father.

It will be very difficult, and sometimes impossible, for a wife to be all she is created to be until her husband becomes all he is supposed to be.

It will be very difficult, and sometimes impossible, for a child to be all he or she is created to be until their father becomes all he is supposed to be. But be encouraged: Many have overcome this situation through Christ!

GOD GIVES US WHAT WE NEED

There is one final concept that is vital for you to take in on this matter of relating as husbands and wives. It is this: *God gives each of us what we NEED to become the people He desires for us to be.*

I said that to my wife one night, "Honey, hear me in the Spirit." I prayed for her and said it again, "Honey, I've had a new insight into God's plan."

She said, "What is it?"

I said, "Now listen in the Spirit. God did not give me the woman I wanted to marry."

Her head spun around and the look she gave me caused every muscle in my body to be ready to duck either to the left or to the right. I said, "No, hear me, now. Hear me. If I had done the choosing, I would have chosen a woman who would have done absolutely everything I wanted her to do all the time and I would have been perfectly happy, comfortable, and not one bit challenged. God had a better idea. He gave me the wife I *needed*."

You see, my wife challenges every weak spot in me and every weak point of my character. She doesn't let me get by with mediocrity — and I'm thankful that she doesn't! She is precisely what I need as a wife. She makes me a better man than I'd be without her.

Let me assure you of this: No matter who you marry, you are not going to find yourself married to the person you *thought* you wanted. But if you are trusting God to lead you into a decision of marriage and trusting Him to cause you to fall in love with His chosen mate for you, then you are going to be living with the person you *need* as a spouse. God is building character in each one of us and He isn't giving up on that challenge. He's put your spouse into your life to help Him in His work!

When you start thinking that the grass is looking greener on the other side of the fence, let me assure you that if you leap over the fence into that pasture, you're going to find God uses that person in an even *stronger* way to give you what you need! Most people I know who leave the spouse they have for someone they think will be "better" find that either they have married the same person in just another form, or they've jumped from the frying pan right into the fire. Why? Because the person doing the leaping hasn't changed. He or she is the same person and still has the same character faults that God is seeking to refine.

Stick with the spouse God gave you! Go together to God and say, "Help us through this hard time. Show us what You are trying to do in each one of us to build our character and make us into the people You want us to be."

Look at each other and say, "Honey, we're going to get through this. We're going to emerge on the other side of this better people — changed, but changed for the better. God is going to do that in us. He's going to make us into people who can be used by Him in a powerful and wonderful way!"

CHAPTER 7

How to Keep the Peace

So much emphasis is placed on problems in marriage, and the story of Samson and Delilah is one that reveals problems, but I believe it's important for us to say that many marriages in our nation today are *good* ones. Not every marriage is in trouble.

Our God is a God of blessing. Just as much as you are called to face up to what may be broken or in need of change in your life, God calls you continually to acknowledge those things that are working, beneficial, and of blessing. Be thankful for the good things He has put in you, done for you, and called you to experience — both individually and as a married couple or family. God has given good gifts to all of us and we must be faithful in our praise to Him!

There are a number of very positive things that every married couple can do to strengthen and build up their marriage. Most of these things are things that can be done on a daily basis — and they are very practical.

There are a number of "top ten" lists in our world today. If I was asked to give you the "top ten things that enrich a marriage," the following would be my list. As you read through these things, keep in mind that these are things you can implement today — right now — whether or not your spouse does them. In fact, I believe if *you* will do them, your marriage will improve, regardless of what your spouse does! These are things that *both* husbands and wives *should* do.

1. FOCUS ON SUCCESSES

Support and encourage what your spouse does right. Don't major on weaknesses, but major on strengths. Become your spouse's greatest fan and most loyal supporter.

Never belittle your spouse, especially in public. Disparaging words and cynicism destroy the heart. They emasculate a man, and they crush a woman.

In contrast, give your spouse high praise for those things that are godly characteristics and noble deeds. Praise your spouse publicly. Words of encouragement, recognition, and appreciation build up a relationship. They make a man stronger, and they make a woman softer.

2. LOVE UNCONDITIONALLY

Don't try to change your spouse. Love what God has created. Neither you nor your spouse are perfect and both of you are going to make mistakes. Unconditional love takes this stance: *nevertheless.*

"You make mistakes, *nevertheless* I love you."

"You have flaws, *nevertheless* I love you."

"You get off track, *nevertheless* I love you."

Choose to love your spouse for who your spouse is before God, without any regard to your spouse's behavior.

A genuine love operates like faith. A genuine love is not based upon feelings any more than it is based upon eyesight and lust. It is a function of your *will* to love. A genuine love operates like faith — some days you don't feel it in your heart, but you know it is there nevertheless. You claim it for yourself. You declare it to be present in you even if you don't feel it.

It's that kind of steadfast love that is required if a marriage is to stay on track. You can't operate by feelings, wishes, desires, signs, or things you can "see." Operate according to your faith that God is in your marriage, He is doing a work in you and your spouse, and He *will* bring it to completion.

There are four things you need to understand about love:

Love suffers long. That means it lasts and it endures, no matter what the other person does or says. Love puts up with circumstances and situations and rides out the storms. Each of us are selfish human beings. In fact, you probably didn't realize how selfish you really were until you got married. Then your selfishness was pointed out to you at every turn!

Part of the process of being married means that selfishness is worn down in us. Over time God heals us of our selfishness. We need to let God work on us so we can get the selfishness out of us.

Love isn't envious or proud. Love doesn't want what the other person has in the way of gifts or position. If a wife truly loves her husband, she won't want his role and all of its responsibilities. She won't be envious of the things the Lord gives to her husband. If a husband truly loves his wife, he won't want to take away her spiritual gifts or strut with pride about the authority God has given to him. Love doesn't lift itself up. As Paul said, **Charity...is not puffed up** (1 Corinthians 13:4).

Love means constant giving. It means that both husband and wife are giving continually. No one person expects to do all the receiving. No one person is expected to do all the changing. What happens in many relationships is that one person is trying to make the other happy, and the other person is taking every piece of happiness they can get. That isn't a genuine loving relationship. Love gives, and gives, and gives.

If you are thinking that when you get married you are going to have someone who will fulfill all of your dreams, meet all of your demands, and provide everything you need, you have some serious "selfishness" issues to work out before you will ever have a successful marriage. Love is about giving and giving and giving. If you don't have that viewpoint about marriage, you are not only going to be sorely frustrated and disappointed, but you may very well be ignored and find that your spouse has turned to someone who is willing to give, rather than demand continually to receive.

Love is not easily provoked. Don't wear your heart on your shirtsleeve. Your love isn't genuine if you are telling your husband one minute that you love him to pieces and then the next minute you are biting his head off. The same goes for husbands who tell their wives how much they love them to get them into bed and then turn right around and criticize them for the least little thing.

The apostle Paul wrote that love **beareth all things, believeth all things, hopeth all things, endureth all things. Charity never faileth** (1 Corinthians 13:7,8). That means you don't get divorced. Love endures. It takes the stance, "We're going to endure this, honey. We're going to come through this rough time. God put us together and we aren't going to let it tear us apart."

3. LISTEN INTENTLY

Every husband needs a wife who will listen to him without criticism, but with support. Every wife needs a husband who will listen to her, patiently and without inserting his judgment. Learn to listen with your heart. Hear the things that are left unsaid, the things that are expressed with a sigh, a tear, a moan, a downcast countenance. Ask sincere questions. Deliver fewer statements. Become an expert at understanding nonverbal communication. Only if you listen intently can you come to an *understanding* of what your spouse is going through and how your spouse is feeling.

4. BE REALISTIC IN YOUR EXPECTATIONS

Don't expect your spouse to meet all of your emotional needs. Some wives expect their husbands to satisfy and fulfill them completely in every area of their life. The same is true for some husbands in their expectations of what a wife will provide for them emotionally. This can't be done. You have emotional, intellectual, and other needs related to your unique gifts and talents that no one person can fill.

Now this certainly isn't a license to have an affair. Your sexual needs *are* to be met by your spouse and your spouse alone. Your deep needs for intimacy and unconditional love are to be filled by your spouse and your spouse alone. But there are other needs for friendship, camaraderie, outlets for creativity, and so forth that your spouse may not be able to fulfill. Seek out good Christian friends, teachers, mentors, companions, colleagues, and partners to fill your life with many satisfying friendships.

5. VALUE YOUR ROLE IN THE RELATIONSHIP

Understand and appreciate the role you play in your spouse's life. If you are being the spouse you are supposed to be in God's plan, nobody else can be who and what you are to your spouse! Nobody can love your spouse like you can. Nobody can do for your spouse what you can do. Nobody can fill the role you play.

Don't belittle your role. Don't relinquish your role. Don't neglect your role. You have the power to crush and destroy the spirit of your spouse like nobody else can. You also have the power to build up, enrich, and assist your spouse like nobody else can. Choose to fulfill your role to the very best of your ability, for the very best benefits in your spouse's life.

Guard your role! Don't let anyone else move in on it.

6. Value Your Spouse as God's Gift

See your spouse as God's gift to you. The Most High and Sovereign God has given you your spouse as His gift to you. Cherish your spouse as your most valued treasure in all of life.

7. Appreciate Your Spouse

Be thankful and appreciative for what your spouse does for you. Be quick to *say* "thank you" to your spouse, not just to feel thankful. Wives, thank your husbands for working all day, for coming home to you night after night, for loving and disciplining your children, for opening doors for you, for standing up for what is good and right in God's eyes.

Husbands, thank your wives for their loyalty to you, for their diligence in training your children, for fixing your meals, for keeping your house, for helping you in your work, for challenging you to be all that you can be in the Lord. Value the little things as well as the big things.

Give genuine compliments. Mean what you say. Say "thank you" from the heart.

8. GIVE YOUR SPOUSE SUFFICIENT SPACE

Nobody thrives if they are smothered. Learn when your spouse needs to be consoled with comforting touches and hugs. Learn when it's best to give your spouse a breath of fresh air. Every person responds to stress in different ways. Some men need a window of time alone so they can sort things out and "collect" themselves. Some women need time alone for reflection and to maintain a quiet spirit before the Lord. Study your own spouse so you can come to an understanding about when to reach out and when to allow your spouse the space required. If in doubt ask, "Do you need to be alone or do you need for me to stay close?"

9. PHYSICALLY APPRECIATE YOUR SPOUSE

No person has a perfect physique. Find the traits in your spouse that are the strongest and compliment them. Every man likes to be told that he is appealing to his wife. Every wife likes to be told that she still is a "turn-on" to her husband.

10. STAY ON THE JOURNEY TOGETHER

Develop a new understanding of your marriage as a journey, not as a destination point. Don't expect your marriage ever to "arrive." You are on a journey together. Enjoy the adventure. Take time to smell the roses along the way. Take time to reflect on your past "good times." Take each other's hand when the way becomes steep or treacherous. Cling together in times of danger and trouble.

LIVING BY CONVICTION, NOT PREFERENCE

We are called to live in a state of marriage according to conviction, not preference. Conviction is rooted in our belief that God is able to resolve any problems that may come in our marriage. When two people live out their marriage by conviction, their marriage gets stronger and stronger. Conviction solidifies their minds and hearts against opposition and pressure.

Preference, however, is when a person chooses to live by "negotiation." One or both parties in the marriage start to live according to what they "prefer" or choose to be the truth rather than to live according to God's truth. They say to themselves, "I'm going to do this according to my preference and desire." A battle of the wills begins — each side negotiating for their preferences. The marriage weakens in the process and may crumble into pieces.

Choose to live by a conviction that as you pursue what is right before God, God will guard you in the right path you walk.

Choose to live by a conviction that as you love unconditionally, God will pour love into your heart.

Choose to live by a conviction that as you listen, God will give you greater understanding and show you even further ways to enhance your marriage.

Choose to live by a conviction that God alone can truly satisfy all of your emotional longings.

Choose to live by a conviction that God has a plan and purpose for you that includes your spouse, who is a great gift of God to you.

Choose to live by a conviction that as you appreciate what your spouse does for you, you will grow in your appreciation for all of life and, in turn, others will appreciate and value you more.

Choose to live by a conviction that as you walk in freedom, you will experience freedom in your spirit even as you fulfill the functional roles God has called you to fill.

Choose to live by the conviction that you can begin to see others as God sees them — from the heart.

Choose to live by the conviction that God will never leave nor forsake your marriage, just as He will never leave nor forsake you.

Walk by conviction and by faith, and your marriage *will* be a good one!

CHAPTER 8

THE RIGHT PROGRESSION OF A GODLY RELATIONSHIP

Agreat deal of damage is done in our world today because people don't understand the nature of how to build or create godly relationships. They don't know how to relate to one another in a godly manner from the outset.

Many people don't know how to develop friendships, much less marriages. We need to take our example from Jesus. He *chose* His friends. Choosing your friends is a part of "guarding your heart," which the Bible tells us to do. Proverbs 4:23 says, **Keep thy heart with all diligence; for out of it are the issues of life.**

Too many of us are getting ourselves hooked into friendships with the wrong people. Then one day we wake up and wonder how we got ourselves into the mess we're in. The problem stems from our lack of understanding about who our friends should be.

Friendships follow a progression which can be likened to the progression of a seed being sown. Unless something abnormal interrupts the progression that comes after a seed is planted, that seed will grow and produce a harvest. If the seed is good, the harvest will be a good one. If the seed is bad, the harvest will still come, but it will be of an undesirable nature. Bad seeds grow by this progression just as much as good seeds do. Jesus spoke about this in a parable:

> **So is the kingdom of God, as if a man should cast seed into the ground;**
>
> **And should sleep, and rise night and day, and the seed should spring and grow up, he knoweth not how.**
>
> **For the earth bringeth forth fruit of herself; first the blade, then the ear, after that the full corn in the ear.**
>
> **But when the fruit is brought forth, immediately he putteth in the sickle, because the harvest is come.**
>
> **Mark 4:26-29**

Every relationship we enter into follows a progression that is just as certain as the growth of a planted seed. *Everything* that is "alive" grows as a seed grows. When you understand how a relationship develops and grows, then you can discern more clearly where you are in the relationships you have "sown."

THE FIVE STAGES OF A RELATIONSHIP

Every relationship follows five stages of development in a precise sequence. These stages progress unless there is a deliberate intervention on your part to stop them.

What we must always be cautious about is moving through these stages too quickly or leaping past some of the stages. For example, a person may have a positive first impression of someone they meet. They immediately begin to imagine what it would be like to be married to that person. The truth is — they don't even *know* that person!

We have had people come for marriage counseling in the church and when they are asked, "How long have you been dating?" they respond, "Oh, we just met a month ago." If the pastor says, "Well, don't you think you need to wait awhile and check each other out?" some of them have responded, "No, we know the Lord put us together. We had signs."

My first impression is, *Yeah, they had signs all right. It's called the lust of the eyes!* They are considering entering into a marriage without adequate information about their intended spouse or how the two of them relate to each other. Later, when their marriage is in trouble, they'll blame it on the Lord — "God put us together and now look what God did!" No, God didn't do anything. He didn't have a *chance* to do anything. They leapfrogged from first date to marriage without going through the normal healthy progression of a relationship.

Progression in a relationship takes time. Just as a healthy, harvest-producing plant doesn't get planted, grow, and produce a harvest in a day, a good, healthy, fruit-producing relationship doesn't happen overnight. I don't care what "signs" you think you had or didn't have.

STAGE #1: FIRST IMPRESSION

This is the introductory stage. Relationships begin when people meet and form an impression of each another. You come together, you see each other, and you go your separate ways. Or you come together, you see each other, and you stick around for more. We all know the phrase, "You never get a second chance to make a first impression." It's a truthful statement.

Impressions are based on outward appearances and behaviors. In the impression stage we make an assessment of what we think the person is like based upon the clothes they are wearing, the way they have put together their overall appearance, the car they are driving, the way they walk and talk, the laugh they have, the things they say, and so forth. Every person majors on different things, different clues as to how they size up a person.

The Bible says that man looks on the outward appearance, but the Lord looks at the heart. (See 1 Samuel 16:7.) It's true. We form our first impression based totally on the outward fleshly appearance and demeanor of a person.

If you like what you see with your eyes, hear with your ears, and feel in your intuition, you have a positive first impression and you then move to the next stage. If you feel repulsed by what you sense, you have a negative impression, move away from them, and don't pursue a relationship. The seed is not allowed to take root.

There are some things that should be definite warning signs to a believer that a first impression should be the last impression. Listen to what the person says. Is every fourth word a swear word or an unclean word? What does the person talk about?

What kind of messages are being sent by the way the person dresses? I'm always amazed at how much "advertising" people do in their choice of clothing. Some women, as well as some men, send strong signals that they are looking for love in all the wrong places.

Don't allow yourself to be enticed by those who send ungodly messages your way. Don't be impressed by their attempt to make an impression on you! Say "no" and walk away in your spirit.

Samson Was Led Astray by What He Saw. Samson's great downfall came when he was led astray by what he saw. And this was long before he ever saw Delilah! I have no idea what the woman from Timnath was wearing or what she looked like. In today's terminology, I imagine she must have been wearing high heels, short shorts, and a halter top, with a figure that caught Samson's full attention. I know women didn't dress that way in Bible times, but however she looked, dressed, walked, and acted — Samson fell for her on the basis of "seeing" her.

So many people get into trouble by acting only on the basis of what they see. They see a new car they can't afford, but what they see sticks in their minds and takes root. They've got to have it, got to have it, got to have it. They end up with a debt they can't pay because they made a decision based on what they saw. The same goes for some people who are buying houses and all sorts of other high-ticket items.

As believers in Christ Jesus, we are to walk by faith in the Word of God and the leading of His Spirit. We are not to get caught up by what we see, but by what we *know* in our spirits to be true and right.

Don't Look Too Long. We can't always avoid seeing evil, or seeing what is enticing in the flesh. But let me give you a little tip: When you see something you know you're not supposed to have or that will lead you into sin, don't look at it long!

If you're single and lonely and you see someone who is extremely good-looking but that person is married, don't look too long. If you come across someone who is truly something to behold with the eyes, but that person is living in sin and not for God, don't look too long. That person is *not* for you!

The longer you look, the more you're going to want, and the more miserable you are going to be. You're going to be miserable if you can't have what you want, and you're going to be even more miserable if you get what you want and it's not of God!

The one thing we know with certainty about all beauty is that it fades. It can be the beauty of a person or the beauty of a flower or the beauty of a sunset, but sooner or later, that beauty fades into oblivion. The person ages, wrinkles form, teeth fall out, the head goes bald, and the body bulges and breaks down in sickness. The flower petals fall off. The sun sets fully into night. Outer beauty never lasts.

Inner beauty lasts and grows. It gets brighter and brighter. Character is the only beauty that has a potential for being even more beautiful fifty years from now than it is today.

Ask God to show you the *real* beauty — beauty you can't see with your physical eyes.

STAGE #2: ACQUAINTANCESHIP

Acquaintanceship is the stage where a person moves beyond an outer assessment and begins to make an inner assessment of another person. There's a seeking for more personal knowledge. We might call it "curiosity." We might call it testing or experimenting. "Half-conversations" begin to occur with lots of questions. When I was in college, my fraternity brothers and I called this the "old hee, hee, ha, ha" stage.

You may be serious in your desire to find out more about the person, but on the other hand, you aren't really serious. You're just testing the other person's attitudes, values, and reactions. For example, a woman might say, "You know, I'd really like to get married and have children." And the man responds, "You know, I really like the single life."

They haven't revealed a lot about themselves, yet they've revealed everything that needs to be said. They've thrown out an opinion, an idea, a wish, a dream, a value. They've "experimented." And in the example I just gave, the experiment showed them exactly what they needed to know. There's no future for a relationship that is not going to be satisfying to either person.

In the acquaintanceship stage, people begin to set boundaries and limitations. They find out where a person is going and if there is any commonality to build upon. Things are very cordial. In fact, things are sometimes overly nice and sweet.

If a person senses agreement at this stage, the relationship can progress. If there is no strong sense of agreement, and especially about things that are highly valued, then the relationship is ended. The seed that sprouted is "nipped off" as soon as it came out of the ground. In Amos 3:3 we read, **Can two walk together, except they be agreed?** The answer is no!

If you discover that the person with whom you are entering into an acquaintanceship has values that differ from those you have as a Christian, that they engage in behaviors you know are ungodly, or that they have dreams and desires that are contrary to the Word of God, there should be no space given to that acquaintanceship. It should not be allowed to progress — I don't care what the person looks like, how fine a first impression they may have made, or how clever the person is at small talk. It doesn't even matter what the person says he or she feels toward you. Give no space to that relationship. If you do, you will quickly find that you are not in agreement.

The greatest power on this earth is to be in agreement with God. If you are in agreement with God and the person with whom you are developing a relationship is in agreement with God, then that relationship truly has the potential to become a threefold cord that will not be easily broken. (See Ecclesiastes 4:12.)

If you and another person do not have agreement about what it means to have a good relationship with God and what it means to live in obedience and to follow Jesus not only as Savior but Lord, you have no choice but to sever the relationship at this stage. You cannot stay in a relationship of strong agreement with God and at the same time enter into a relationship with a person who is rebellious or indifferent toward God or who chooses to remain alienated from God.

On the other hand, if you sense this agreement, as well as agreement on other things that you like and dislike as individuals, then you probably will move on to the next stage of the relationship. You'll have a *desire* to learn more about the person and to spend more time with the person because there's something cooking between the two of you, something is clicking, something is "happening."

STAGE #3: DEEPER DISCLOSURE

The third phase in the progression of a relationship is deeper disclosure. At this stage, people begin sharing private information with another person — deeper insights into self, family, friends, frustrations, prayer needs, prejudices, desires, hopes, things that cause discomfort or pain. The more of this type of information that is shared, the greater the potential for trust.

This stage requires a high degree of vulnerability. Most people remember their first loves very fondly because their "first love" was the relationship in which they moved into this disclosure stage for the first time. It was the first time they shared their secret feelings with another person. It was the first time they were vulnerable to another person and trusted another person with their previously unspoken desires, hopes, and dreams for love.

If you truly want to get close to another person, you are going to have to trust a person with what you consider to be private feelings and thoughts. Disclosure is the foundation on which trust is built.

This is true also in the spirit realm. It is when we disclose our innermost feelings, desires, and longings to God that an intimacy develops with God. In return, God begins to disclose to us more about His awesome nature, His unconditional and everlasting love, and His trust in us to carry His Word to others. Our feelings for God become more intense and we long to spend more time with Him.

What happens if trust is violated and vulnerability is betrayed? The relationship ends at this point. The seed has sprouted and begun to branch out, but it is pulled from the ground by its roots if trust is violated.

Don't continue in a relationship where your disclosure is dismissed casually, discussed freely with others, or gossiped about. Don't continue in a relationship where you are continually wondering what the other person may be doing with your secrets and your confessions of love. If you cannot trust a person at the disclosure stage, you will not be able to trust that person in the next two stages of a relationship.

STAGE #4: FRIENDSHIP

The next stage in the building of a relationship is genuine friendship. This stage is generally characterized not only by a great deal of trust and disclosure, but also by faithfulness and a high degree of expectation. This change may be subtle, but it is actually very substantive.

The more disclosure that occurs, the stronger the base of trust, and the more the desire to continue in a relationship, then the more the "expectation level" rises. You begin to expect the other person to be there for you when you need them. You count on spending time with them, communicating openly with them and doing things spontaneously to encourage and express concern for each other.

As you spend time together, communicate with each other, and give to each other, people who are outside your relationship will begin to notice. The relationship takes on a special meaning in part because others know and label you as friends. They are no longer surprised to see you together and they actually come to expect you to be together.

If you are in a romantic relationship, then you are perceived as "going together." If you are in a business relationship, then you are perceived to be "partners." If you are in a church relationship, then you are "fellow believers." If you are in a social relationship, then you are perceived as good friends, buddies, confidants. When friendship develops, two people begin to spend time with other friends who are like them. They develop a circle of friends.

At this point, if you have allowed an ungodly relationship to develop, you will find it difficult to extract yourself because you will find yourself outnumbered. No longer will it just be you and the other person, but you and the other person and a whole lot of people who are just like that other person!

In friendship, you begin to be able to anticipate and to explain the behavior of your friend. In many friendships, one person actually begins to be able to complete the sentences started by the other person.

A closeness develops in friendship that keeps each person from change, to a degree. Friendship is built upon commonalties, upon disclosure, upon trust, upon shared experiences. Some change and growth are possible, but to some extent, those things that brought the friends together are likely to be the things that keep the friends together.

If you find yourself in a friendship in which your friend does not allow you to grow in the Lord, or criticizes any desire you have for more of God, you must back away from the friendship and give it less space. The seed may have sprouted into a wonderful vine or tree, but it needs to be severely pruned if the desire of one friend is that the other person cease to grow spiritually.

If friendship continues and is enriching to both parties, with sufficient room to grow spiritually and to continue to develop as a person toward wholeness and excellence, then the friendship is likely to progress to the fifth and final stage.

STAGE #5: FORMALIZATION

In formalization, there is an announcement of some kind to the world at large that you have and expect to continue your relationship. If the relationship is a romantic one, the relationship is formalized in marriage — a wedding is announced, a family is formed. If the relationship is in the business realm, a partnership is announced and the association is given a formal birth, generally including business cards and signs.

If the relationship is one involving the church, a membership is announced to the congregation as a whole. If the relationship is social, then somehow the word is spread that you are good friends, lifelong friends, best of friends, and so forth. People know that you are in relationship and that you both want that relationship to continue.

You are not only willing for this announcement to be public, but you are proud of it. You have no qualms about people knowing that you are friends, partners, members of a church, or married. To a great extent, you are willing for your relationship to be assessed by others. You are not ashamed that you are a friend, partner, member, or spouse.

In the spirit realm, a person who comes to Jesus Christ and accepts Him as Savior and Lord is a person who has moved through these five stages of relationship to the point where they are willing to declare to the world, "Jesus is my Savior. He is my Lord. I am a Christian." The person has had a favorable impression of Jesus, has moved into an acquaintanceship with Him, and has pursued a time of learning more about Him.

The more Jesus Christ is revealed, the deeper the trust level and the awareness of His love. The more this happens, the more the person realizes that

Jesus offers genuine and eternal friendships — He, indeed, is the Friend Who will always stick closer than any brother or sister. As the person yields more and more to Christ, the relationship is eventually formalized. The genuine born-again Christian will never be ashamed to say, "I belong to Jesus Christ." The relationship is formalized in a confession about Him even if a church membership hasn't happened yet.

PRIORITIES IN RELATIONSHIPS

The amount of space that you give to your formalized friendships is determined by the importance of the relationship to your life. And here is where we must be very aware that God has set priorities for our relationships.

A formalized relationship with Jesus Christ is the most important relationship you can have and the relationship that needs to be given the most space in your life. Your relationships with your spouse and your children are to be more important than any other human relationship you have. Your family members are to be more important to you than any friendship or business relationship.

And finally, some friends are to be more important to you than others. You may have a disciple friend, someone you are mentoring. You may have a close confidant friend, someone in whom you confide your secrets. You may have a casual friend, someone with whom you can shop or have lunch. These friendships should be prioritized according to two factors:

Friendships should be prioritized according to spiritual maturity. Spend time with those friends who also consider their relationship with Jesus Christ to be the central relationship of their lives. You will have far more in common with those friends than with those who are less mature in their love for the Lord. You will learn more from them and have a greater bond of trust with them than with friends who are spiritually immature.

Friendships should be prioritized according to the degree to which the two of you can share the things of God. Your best friends should be those with whom you can talk freely about the Word of God, pray, praise, engage in Christian ministry, and attend church-related events and retreats together. Choose friends who are headed in the same direction you are headed — in other words, friends who are on the path to heaven and desire your companionship along the way.

Every relationship occupies a space in your life, but there is only so much space you have available for other people. Relationships take time, effort, thought, care, concern, and expressions of giving. All of these "requirements" are the space needed to maintain a good relationship. Some relationships require more space than others to keep them nourished and flourishing.

We each need to be aware that a marriage needs a great deal of space. Children need a great deal of space. Good, deep, and lasting friendships require space, but that space should be less than the space allotted to marriage and children. Acquaintanceships require less space than friendships.

Jesus had this understanding. Of all those who followed Him, He chose twelve to be His close friends. And among those twelve, He chose Peter, James, and John to be with Him in the most significant moments of His life.

You will be confronted from time to time by people who want more space in your life than you either can or should give to them. If you don't have an understanding about relationships, you may be tempted to give them that space, and if you do and they are not worthy of that space, you later will have difficulty because you will need to limit their space. Feelings will be hurt. The fact is, you should never have allowed the person to move into such a large space in your life.

People will take advantage of you if they can. Be aware of that. They will want to sap the affection and caring that you have. If you allow it, you will be taking the affection and care that rightfully belong to your spouse and children and giving it to other relationships that are demanding unrightfully of you.

Lots of people are being used up by "zeroes" — people who should have *zero* space in their life.

These are people you shouldn't even have as acquaintances, much less friends. These people should be "off limits" to you, other than to greet them politely in social settings or to give them a word of witness about Jesus Christ. Zeroes are people who are living in sin or are enticing you to engage in sin. They are people who want to move in on the important relationships in your life — your relationship with the Lord, your relationship with your spouse or children — and claim an undeserved and unrighteous space in your life. They want to manipulate you and influence you for their own purposes.

THE DEATH OF A RELATIONSHIP

Relationships begin to deteriorate at any stage when you begin to magnify your differences. If you see major differences at the first impression stage, the relationship dies quickly. In fact, it never takes root. If you see major differences at the acquaintanceship stage, you probably won't pursue the relationship to the disclosure stage, and so forth.

What happens after a relationship has moved through these five stages, has been formalized, and then differences arise? What should you do? Some differences are normal. They should be expected. The first thing you should decide is not to panic. Differences do not spell doom or the demise of a relationship. *Lifting up differences* and making a big deal of them is what leads to destruction of a relationship.

Most differences that occur after friendships have developed and a relationship has been formalized are probably not major differences unless, of course, the person has been a master of deceit all along the way. Differences generally emerge over time in the natural course of getting to know a person. If a person gives a relationship sufficient time to progress through the first four stages in a normal manner, any differences that are significant will usually surface, and then at that point a person will have to ask, "Is this really important to me? Can I live with this?"

If the answer is "No, I can't live with this — this is too important for me to overlook or to compromise my values," the relationship should be dissolved, no matter how much time has been invested up to that stage of disclosure or friendship. If the answer is "Yes, I can live with this — it isn't all that big a deal," then the relationship can progress to formalization.

Never assume that once a relationship has been formalized, you will be able to change the other person and the differences that bother you will be erased! It won't happen.

That's one of the reasons I counsel young people to spend considerable time getting to know the person they are beginning to anticipate marrying. Get to know that person. It's far better to call off a friendship, even an engagement, than to end up in a miserable, maladjusted, and misaligned marriage.

Once a relationship has been formalized, most differences that emerge aren't likely to be major ones. They should be ignored, dismissed, laughed at, and even appreciated, but not emphasized! Some things just don't deserve to have the spotlight turned on them. There's a lot of truth in the old saying, "Don't turn a molehill into a mountain."

Jesus said this a different way, **How wilt thou say to thy brother, Let me pull out the mote out of thine eye; and, behold, a beam is in thine own eye?** (Matthew 7:4). Let motes go without comment. Work on your own relationship with the Lord and the pursuit of excellence of your own character. Flaws in others are *not* a territory over which you have been given the right to judge.

Don't lift up your differences so high that you trip over them!

When differences are emphasized, the communication turns negative. Suddenly, all you are talking about are your differences, then you are talking about the problems caused by your differences, and then you are talking about the problems that are being caused by the fact that you have so many problems!

Don't allow yourself to harp on the differences you see in your relationship. If you do, you will likely never let go of those differences. You'll bring them up in next week's argument, and then in next month's argument. Pretty soon the differences will solidify into "you always" and "you never" statements. The differences themselves become entrenched and tear a relationship down to a level where trust is destroyed, vulnerability is sealed off, and time spent together is eroded.

What should you do instead? Continue to emphasize those things that brought you together and which you hold in common. When the Lord is common ground between you, place your greatest emphasis on the agreement you have in the Spirit. Talk about Jesus. Talk about the Word of God. Talk about the good things God has done, is doing, and which you believe He will do for you, your marriage, your children, and in turn, through your family for your church and for the world.

Talk about the things you have and enjoy doing together. Talk about your good memories of happy times in the past. Establish and practice customs that are unique to your family — things that can make happy memories for your children. Magnify the Lord in each other! Talk about the good things you see the Lord doing in your spouse and through your spouse. Build each other up.

Your marriage will never grow beyond needing to be bolstered, enriched, and nurtured by placing an emphasis on your commonalties and your mutual love for Jesus Christ. A strong foundation must continually be built upon and strengthened. In that way, relationships not only flourish, but they grow, deepen, and expand. Then years from now you can look back and say, "I love you so much more now. I thought I loved you with my whole heart, but my heart has expanded, and I love you with an even much bigger heart."

Isn't that the type of relationship we all long to have — a relationship that is growing and is becoming ever more meaningful and more characteristic of Jesus' unbounded love? You can have that type of relationship, but you must build slowly, steadily, and wisely, always sensitive to what God is desiring to do for you. Never settle for less than God's best for you!

If God has given you a heart's desire to be married, then He has a spouse in mind for you. Wait for Him to reveal His "best person" to you. If your heart's deep desire is to have a friend or a partner in business, then God has the right person for you. Trust Him and trust His timing. Allow time for God to grow the harvest of a "good relationship" in your life.

NEVER STOP COMMUNICATING

If commonalties are what leads to a good formalized relationship, then communication is the lifeblood of that good relationship. Any relationship that begins to deteriorate is nearly always marked by a breakdown in communication. When communication ceases, is incomplete, or is rooted in hatred, an atmosphere of confusion and distrust develops.

When confusion and distrust mark a relationship, the relationship will die unless the confusion is cleared up and trust can be reestablished. If the relationship is a marriage, unresolved confusion and distrust will result in divorce. Many reasons may be given for a couple divorcing, but in virtually all cases I've witnessed, there has been a marked lack of communication, a great deal of confusion, and a significant amount of distrust.

If the relationship is in the church, confusion, distrust, and a lack of communication can result in members leaving and a church dissolving. If the relationship is in business, unresolved communication difficulties will create a confusion and distrust that ends in partnerships being dissolved, customers being dissatisfied, and vendors failing to provide needed resources. The business will fail.

No matter how tough a problem may be or how difficult the circumstances in your relationships, keep communicating! To fail to communicate is to set the stage for confusion and distrust. The moment you stop talking, fragmentation begins to set in and if it isn't corrected, the demise of the relationship begins and can result in the death of that relationship.

GOD'S DESIRE

Never lose sight of the fact that God *desires* for you to be in godly relationships with other people. He is the One Who "grows" a relationship; the plan is His. He will give you the discernment you need to determine which people are being placed into your life by Him as your friends, colleagues, partners, associates, clients, and customers. He is the One Who will bring you your spouse. Trust Him!

I have heard a number of single people moan, "I want to be married and there's nobody to marry." Let me assure you of this: If God has given you a deep desire to be married, then He has someone in mind for you to marry. Trust Him to reveal that person to you. Don't jump for the first person who comes your way. Take time to get to know a person. Let a relationship develop according to God's natural progression for a healthy marriage. Be confident and expectant in your spirit that God *does* have someone for you to marry and He *will* bring that person your way.

You may have to get beyond your own expectations about how your future spouse will look or act. You may have to die to some of your own fantasies about how much money your future husband will have or the figure of your future wife. Nevertheless, God has a person for you who is *right* for you — someone who will truly be a good husband for YOU or be a good wife for YOU.

CHAPTER 9

SEX IS FOR MARRIAGE *ONLY*

S ome people have gotten so far out of God's will that they are perishing. They are perishing for their lack of knowledge of God. They don't know that's why they are perishing, but the reason is simple: They are in disobedience to God's commands and ignorant of God's plans.

One of those areas of disobedience in our society — an area that is rampantly out of control — is the area of sexual relationships. In Genesis 4:1 we read,

And Adam knew Eve his wife; and she conceived, and bare Cain, and said, I have gotten a man from the Lord.

"Knew" in this context means to have sexual intercourse. Rightly understood, sex is knowing a person at the deepest level possible, at the maximum level of intimacy. From God's viewpoint, to have sexual intercourse with a person is to "know" that person in all dimensions. Sexual intercourse is intended by God to be an act that is enjoyed within the context of the commitment of marriage, and *only* within the context of marriage.

In this one verse we have two very important principles:

Marriage is to be the ONLY context for sexual intimacy. Eve was Adam's *wife* — not his girlfriend, his mistress, or a casual acquaintance. He was *married* to her.

Most people who read or study the Bible tend to skip over the chapters that are filled with genealogy — the "begats" — the chapters that give the lineage of a tribe, family, or person. One of the important things we must recognize about the genealogies, however, is that all of those people were *married*. Their children were born within the context of marriage.

Children are to be conceived ONLY within the sexual intimacy of marriage. When Adam and Eve had sex, they created a baby. Now certainly that doesn't mean that the first time they had sex they created Cain. It means that the outcome of their sexual relationship was a child.

Those two statements of principle about marriage may seem obvious to you, but look around you and you'll quickly conclude that most of the world doesn't live by these principles. You can hardly see a commercial or an advertisement today in which sex isn't being used to sell a product. You can hardly see a movie which doesn't have an impure sexual relationship, including a lot of the movies that supposedly are acceptable for children to see. Neither Madison Avenue nor Hollywood live according to God's plan, so neither will present God's plan to others!

Magazines, TV drama shows, TV situation comedies, talk shows, paperback novels, music videos, and MTV all tell the story — people in our culture are "knowing" too many people. In our society, sexual intercourse is not limited to marriage. As a result, millions of babies are being conceived each year outside the context of marriage.

VIRGINS UNTIL MARRIAGE

The Bible standard is that men and women are to be virgins until they are married. Any time this doesn't occur in the Bible, the incident is considered to be rape. Now it is not just women who are to be virgins, but men *and* women. There's no double standard allowed — that men get to sow their wild oats and only women must keep themselves pure. The fact is, men *are* sowing wild oats. The oats they are sowing turn out to be *wild!*

We are in great error when we wink and laugh about the sexual exploits of a young man, as if he has done something great. If a man brags about having so-called "casual sex" with a woman, he is under the judgment of God because he has brought shame to what God has ordained. In truth, he is operating outside God's plan and the outcome is not only going to be damaging to him personally in his spirit, but to his future marriage.

I'm not just talking about AIDS or sexually transmitted diseases when I refer to damage. I'm talking about emotional and spiritual damage — the inability to commit and to connect, the inability to experience true intimacy, the inability to give one's self wholly to another person because part of you has already been given away.

Which parent is responsible for the virginity of their sons and daughters? Fathers primarily, and mothers secondarily. Now that is a message that is going to slap some of you very hard. You may never have heard that message stated so explicitly and directly.

In Deuteronomy 22:13-15,17-21 (NKJV) we read how serious virginity was considered by God:

> **If any man takes a wife, and goes in to her, and detests her, and charges her with shameful conduct, and brings a bad name on her, and says, "I took this woman, and when I came to her I found she was not a virgin," then the father and mother of the young woman shall take and bring out the evidence of the young woman's virginity to the elders of the city at the gate.**
>
> **And they shall spread the cloth before the elders of the city. Then the elders of that city shall take that man and punish him; and they shall fine him one hundred shekels of silver and give them to the father of the young woman, because he has brought a bad name on a virgin of Israel. And she shall be his wife; he cannot divorce her all his days.**
>
> **But if the thing is true, and evidences of virginity are not found for the young woman, then they shall bring out the young woman to the door of her father's house, and the men of**

**her city shall stone her to death with stones,
because she has done a disgraceful thing in
Israel, to play the harlot in her father's house.
So you shall put away the evil from among you.**

How many women today would live past their
wedding day? If a woman in the time of Moses was
found *not* to be a virgin, she was stoned on the day
after her wedding! The biggest fear many people
today have about sexual promiscuity is whether
they will get caught by someone or catch a fatal
disease. The bigger fear should be the fear of God.

THE BLOOD COVENANT

We need to understand that sex is directly
related to forming a blood covenant with another
person. From the Bible's standpoint, a blood
covenant is a very serious matter. When the hymen
of a woman is penetrated for the first time, there is
a shedding of blood. That shed blood is the "token"
of her virginity — evidence to all the world that
she was a virgin.

In Bible times, the family of the bride wanted to
see the sheet of the bed after a marriage had been
consummated. The blood on the sheet was the
evidence that their daughter had been a virgin at the
time of her wedding. The shedding of that blood as
it flows over the man's penis is a sign before God
that the man and the woman have entered into a
sacred blood covenant relationship.

In essence, when you "know" a virgin outside
the context of marriage, you are still saying to God,
"I'm marrying this person," just as if you had gone

through a ceremony, made vows, exchanged rings, and cut a cake.

The Bible's standard for sex is that it be a total-person experience. Sex is to be in the context of desiring to understand everything about a person. You can't possibly understand everything about a person after spending two hours with them in the back seat of a car.

Sex is far more than a physical act. It is the creation of an emotional and spiritual bond. We tend to realize this most when a marriage is in trouble. If there's a breakdown in the sexual relationship between a husband and wife, it is always after they have had an intellectual and emotional breakdown in their marriage. They have stopped communicating, stopped caring, stopped showing affection in little ways. Sexual problems rarely cause emotional and intellectual break-downs, but emotional and intellectual breakdowns in a relationship always cause problems in the sexual relationship.

You might be saying, "But I only meant it as a physical act." That doesn't matter. What you meant and what the reality was before God are two different things. You might not have *meant* to fall off a mountain when you stepped over the edge of a cliff, but you fell nevertheless.

Many people simply do not understand that even though they may have disconnected physically from a person, they may still be connected soulishly (emotionally) and spiritually to that person. The only way they can truly be free from that entanglement is to experience forgiveness and cleansing from God for their sexual sin.

Furthermore, when you sleep with someone, you're sleeping with everyone they have slept with before. There's a connection. Physicians verify this. Bacteria and disease linger long after a physical relationship is broken off — in some cases, years and decades. Beyond that, there's a spiritual connection and a soulish connection that are unseen. There are memories of what those other people were like. There is emotional pain and guilt about what it was like to be joined together and then to be separated from that person. There's a hardness of heart because you have come to use people for your own pleasure as if they were playthings. Even if you don't *feel* guilty, you are guilty before God, and true joy in a sexual relationship cannot take place in the presence of guilt.

UNDERSTANDING SEXUAL SIN

There's a lot of talk today about what is the compassionate thing to do, the "loving" thing to do, the "politically correct" thing to do. I'm concerned about what is the Bible thing to do! God has made His opinion about sexual relationships very clear to us. He gives us a choice to obey or to disobey, but He does not give us a choice to change His rules or to negotiate His standards. The Bible teaching on sexual sin couldn't be stated any clearer than it is in 1 Corinthians 6:9,10:

Know ye not that the unrighteous shall not inherit the kingdom of God? Be not deceived: neither fornicators, nor idolaters, nor adulterers, nor effeminate, nor abusers of themselves with mankind...shall inherit the kingdom of God.

Fornicators are single people who have sexual intercourse outside the bonds of marriage.

Adulterers are those who have sexual intercourse with a married person who is not their own spouse. If a married person has sex with a married person who is not their spouse or with a single person, they are an adulterer. If a single person has sex with a married person, they are an adulterer.

Effeminate and abusers of themselves with mankind refers to homosexuals. They are having sex outside the bonds of marriage because the Bible has no provision for two people of the same sex to be married. Two people of the same sex cannot multiply physically or spiritually. They cannot reproduce in the physical, natural realm, which is an outward manifestation of their inability to produce the fruit of righteousness in the spirit realm.

One of the things we are wise to recognize as we face the issue of sexual promiscuity and talk to our children about sexual relationships is this: The devil is a liar about everything, but particularly when it comes to sex! And the devil specializes in half-truths.

The devil will tell you that sex is ALWAYS fun. Within the context of marriage sex is fun, but outside of marriage it brings guilt, and guilt is never fun. Any time there is an element of abuse or misuse, sex is not enjoyable to the one being abused or misused.

The devil will tell you that everyone is having sex so it must be all right for YOU to have sex. The fact is, it doesn't matter to God if the vast majority of people you know are having sexual intercourse with half the school or half the neighborhood. It doesn't matter if some people within the church are sexually promiscuous. It doesn't matter what your mother and father might do, or what your brothers and sisters might do. It doesn't matter if people make fun of you or tease you about your virginity.

What matters is what God thinks. What matters is whether you are faithful to God. Those who are faithful to God are the ones who are in the position to receive His greatest blessings as they enter marriage.

The devil will tell you that since you are doing everything ELSE right, it is all right for you to sin in this one area. God doesn't grade on the curve, as many people seem to think. Even in the Church there are people who hold the opinion, "Well, I'm living pretty holy in 80 percent of my life and only about 20 percent of my life isn't right, so I'm doing better than I was. Surely God will be pleased with that." Others say to themselves, "This area of sex is the only area of sin in my life and that's pretty good."

Wrong! God doesn't wink at your sin because it's your only sin. Sin is sin. It is destructive to your relationship with God, it can keep God's blessing off your life, and if it goes unrepented, it *will* be deadly to you spiritually and perhaps physically. The Bible says very clearly, "All sin stinks in the nostrils of God." (See Amos 4:10.)

Don't deceive yourself in this! Sexual immorality is sexual immorality no matter what else may be "right" in your life.

The devil will tell you that sexual needs are just like any other needs, so God must expect you to satisfy them. One of the lies the devil has told us is that sexual needs are just like any other physical needs. If you're hungry, you drop by a fast-food restaurant and get a hamburger with cheese. If you're thirsty, you get a drink of water. If you feel a need for sex, get a date with a willing person.

No! Sexual needs are not the same as other physical needs. You need air to breathe, water to drink, and food to eat to *survive* as a physical being. As much as you may think to the contrary, you do not *need* sex to survive as a human being. There are lots of celibate people on the earth today who are very healthy, happy, and fulfilled — physically, emotionally, and spiritually.

The apostle Paul wrote:

> **Meats for the belly, and the belly for meats: but God shall destroy both it and them. Now the body is not for fornication, but for the Lord; and the Lord for the body.**
>
> **1 Corinthians 6:13**

There is a huge difference between your stomach being hungry and your hormones being "hungry"! Paul very plainly states that the body is the temple of the Holy Spirit. Once we have accepted Jesus Christ into our lives, our body is no longer "ours," to do with as we please. Read what he wrote in 1 Corinthians 6:19,20:

> **What? know ye not that your body is the temple of the Holy Ghost which is in you, which ye have of God, and ye are not your own?**
>
> **For ye are bought with a price: therefore glorify God in your body, and in your spirit, which are God's.**

The body was not created to serve sex. Sex was made to enhance a marriage relationship and to bring fulfillment to husband and wife as a means of "knowing" one another. Sex was made to serve a marriage.

The devil will tell you that God MADE you with a strong sex drive or a homosexual orientation that is uncontrollable by your will. No! Some people are quick to offer this excuse for their sexual behavior: "God made me this way. He made me with these strong feelings and desires." No, God didn't make you that way. You may have the desires, but God gave you a strong, free will to govern how you behave and how you act on the drives and desires of the flesh! *Every* person has been given a free will to act as they choose to act. Your sexual behavior is subject to your will. You can *decide* that you will not sin sexually.

If you have strong sexual desires, God has a way for you to express those desires that is morally right. If you have not met the one He has for you to marry and express your sexual longings in that way, you must allow God to give you the grace and courage *not* to sin by pouring your sexual energy into other activities that are productive for God's kingdom.

Neither does God *make* a person to be a homosexual. Look at yourself naked in a mirror and see what God gave you. That's who you *are* in God's creation. Your parents, your grandparents, your peers, or someone else may have influenced you to engage in sexual behavior that was not godly, but *God* did not ordain that behavior for you. God's plan is for sex to be between man and woman in the context of marriage, for pleasure and for the ultimate purpose of bearing children.

SEXUAL SIN CAN BE FORGIVEN!

I certainly am not saying all of this to you to make you feel guilty or condemned. If you have been washed by the blood of Jesus and have been sanctified and made holy by the presence of the Holy Spirit in you, then you are in the category of "I used to have that lifestyle."

Read what Paul wrote to the Corinthians *after* telling them that fornicators, idolaters, adulterers, "abusers of themselves with mankind," thieves, covetous, drunkards, revilers, and extortioners would not inherit the kingdom of God:

> **And such were some of you: but ye are washed, but ye are sanctified, but ye are justified in the name of the Lord Jesus, and by the Spirit of our God.**
>
> **1 Corinthians 6:11**

There's good news! You don't have to BE what you WERE. Your past doesn't need to dictate your future. You can be forgiven and cleansed completely from your old sexual sins. The only way to disconnect from someone with whom you have had sex outside the bonds of marriage is to experience the regeneration of Jesus Christ, Who forgives and cleanses and heals.

The wonderful news for you is this: What God forgives, He forgives completely. He also *forgets*. He throws your confessed sins into His sea of forgetfulness and He never brings up your past sins to accuse you. (See Hebrews 8:12 and 10:17.) Follow His example in your attitude toward yourself. If you have confessed your sin and been forgiven of it, leave it behind you. Don't dwell on it. Don't continue to beat yourself up over it. If your spouse has had a sexually impure background and been forgiven, don't beat them up either. Move forward in your life and marriage in forgiveness.

If you were sexually misused in the past, as the victim of incest or rape, then go to God and ask Him to cleanse and heal you of the memories and harmful effects of that experience. Trust Him to deliver you from the bondage you have felt regarding that abuser. Receive His forgiveness and then forgive yourself and your offender completely. Don't allow a "false guilt" and bitterness to trap you.

If you are a virgin today, keep yourself. Stay a virgin until you marry. If you have sinned in this area, go to God and ask for His forgiveness. Ask Him to cleanse you of that sin and to heal you so you can enter a marriage as an emotionally and spiritually whole person. If you are married and you have sinned with a person other than your spouse, you must also ask God to forgive you and cleanse you of that sin if you are to ever have any hope of getting your marriage fully on track with God's plan. And then, once you have received God's forgiveness, keep yourself pure.

How to Remain Pure

There are four practical things you can do to remain pure before God:

1. Know your own limits and don't tempt yourself by testing them. Know yourself well enough to know what you can and cannot see without burning up with lust. Don't tempt yourself.

I recently heard about a man and a woman who called themselves friends and roommates. They were sharing a house, but they slept in separate rooms and thought this was just fine. Besides having the appearance of evil, I made a suggestion to them: "You are human. Get out of this situation. You are tempting yourselves to do something you both say you don't want to do."

Face up to your own weaknesses and ask God to give you the strength to walk away from something that might only be a little bit tempting. If you know you have a weakness for chocolate ice cream and you see the chocolate ice cream truck coming down the street, you are foolish to wait for it to pull up right in front of you. It doesn't matter if you are saying to yourself, "I'm strong, I'm on a diet, I'm not going to touch any of this." If that ice cream truck stays parked there long enough, you'll be licking a chocolate ice cream cone! Don't subject yourself to that same kind of temptation regarding sex.

Paul said very plainly to the Corinthians: **Flee fornication** (1 Corinthians 6:18). Don't stand around waiting to see what will happen or experiment with how "strong" you might be. In the end, you will become weaker than you ever thought possible.

2. Arm yourself with the Word of God. God has made His Word available to us as a powerful sword against the temptations of the devil. (See Ephesians 6:17.) To properly use the Word of God against sexual temptation, however, you need to *know* the Word of God and have it in your heart so you can quickly call it to mind and quote it aloud to the enemy.

> **Put on the whole armour of God, that ye may be able to stand against the wiles of the devil....**
>
> **And take the helmet of salvation, and the sword of the Spirit, which is the word of God.**
>
> **Ephesians 6:11,17**

If you are continually tormented by sexual feelings, then you need to face up to the fact that you are being *spiritually lazy.* You have not stored up the Word of God in you so you can use the Word against the devil every time he comes at you to try to get you to sin. You may need to use the Word dozens of times before the devil will leave you alone, but in the end, he will flee from you and from the presence of the Word. He fled from Jesus when Jesus used the Word against him during His time of temptation in the wilderness. (See Matthew 4:1-11.)

> **Submit yourselves therefore to God. Resist the devil, and he will flee from you.**
>
> **Draw nigh to God, and he will draw nigh to you. Cleanse your hands, ye sinners; and purify your hearts, ye double minded.**
>
> **James 4:7,8**

When we resist the devil with the Word and seek to draw nigh to God, the devil *will* flee from us and God *will* draw close to us. We do not need to be hounded continually by sexual fantasies or lustful desires. We can be free of that temptation if we will only do what the Bible tells us to do.

3. Choose to think about something else. We each have the ability to govern what we will think about, what we will dwell on, and what we will fantasize about. If you are a single person, govern your thoughts about sex.

If I was face-to-face with you today and I said to you, "Now, don't think about an elephant. You know, the creature with big ears and a long trunk and treelike legs. You know, the big gray creatures with long tusks that live in Africa. Don't think about an elephant. In fact, it's a sin to think about an elephant. No matter what I say, don't think about one. Don't, don't, don't!" What are you going to be thinking about? An elephant!

Don't continually say to your child, "Don't have sex." Get your child thinking about something else. If you are single, don't dwell continually on the fact that you don't have a sexual relationship. Think about something else!

4. Ask God to help you stay pure. If you will make a commitment to God to stay pure sexually, God will help you to fulfill that commitment. The Holy Spirit has been given to you for just that purpose — to help you obey what you know is right before God. The Holy Spirit will empower you to say no to temptation and to resist the devil's attempts to destroy you. The Holy Spirit will wash your mind continually so you will not dwell on every sexual connotation that comes before you.

It is not enough to *know* God's truth. We must be *doers* of the truth. (See James 1:23.) Trust God to give you the courage you need to live a life of sexual purity.

CHAPTER 10

BREAKING DESTRUCTIVE PATTERNS

S amson was so ripe for a fall that Delilah really didn't have to do all that much. She just had to be there at the right time and say the right words over and over again. You see, Delilah was not the *first* or *only* detour Samson took away from God's plan. Delilah was not the first time Samson "messed up." The real story of Samson and Delilah actually began twenty years before Delilah showed up.

One of the worst things any person can do is to attempt to cover up the mistakes of their past and to pretend those mistakes never happened, or to justify those mistakes as being unimportant and inconsequential. It's always a mistake to say, "I have never sinned." God's Word clearly says, **If we say that we have no sin, we deceive ourselves, and the truth is not in us** (1 John 1:8).

It is an equal mistake to say, "That mistake in my past wasn't important and has no bearing on my present or my future." The seeds of disobedience in our past are seeds we must reckon with and face squarely. If we don't own up to our past mistakes and call them for the sins they were, we are in grave danger of committing those same sins again. The more we sin, the less likely we are to call our behavior sin. Pretty soon, we have no conscience left as to what is right or wrong. When that happens, we are so deeply deceived that we may never be able to see the light of God's truth.

SAMSON'S PATTERN OF REBELLION AND ANGER

Samson's first mistake came when he went down to Timnath and he **saw a woman in Timnath of the daughters of the Philistines** (Judges 14:1). Samson wandered over into enemy territory and saw a woman he wanted. How many men make that initial mistake today! They wander outside the church into the territory of the world and they see a woman they desire.

Samson came home and told his father and mother that he had seen the girl of his dreams. He then said to them, **Now therefore get her for me to wife** (Judges 14:2). Even when they protested, Samson insisted.

It was the custom of that time for parents to arrange marriages for their children. Samson really couldn't have arranged his marriage to this girl on his own. Often money or other family goods and property exchanged hands at the time of a marriage. Samson came home and told his parents that he wanted them to secure this enemy Philistine girl as his wife and he insisted that they follow his wishes.

Samson's initial error was twofold. First, he chose a girl who was from the enemy camp. Second, he disobeyed his parents, who knew this girl wasn't right for him and strongly objected — not because she was of a different race, but because she was of a people who worshipped other gods. God forbid Israelites to marry those who did not serve Him. So Samson's insistence on marrying this girl was an act of rebellion against his parents and against God.

But the error didn't stop there. Samson went on to "negotiate" with the enemy. After he had killed the lion that roared against him in Timnath, he told neither his mother nor his father what had happened. In the days that followed that incident, Samson had an opportunity to walk by the carcass of the lion he had killed and he saw that a swarm of honey bees had set up residence in the carcass. He fended off the bees and took some of the honey for himself and his parents, but again, he didn't tell his parents the source of the honey.

As a part of the festivities leading up to his wedding with the young woman from Timnath, Samson held a feast for the young men of the area. About thirty men showed up and Samson said to them,

> **I will now put forth a riddle unto you: if ye can certainly declare it me within the seven days of the feast, and find it out, then I will give you thirty sheets and thirty change of garments:**

> But if ye cannot declare it me, then shall ye give
> me thirty sheets and thirty change of garments.
> And they said unto him, Put forth thy riddle,
> that we may hear it.

> **Judges 14:12,13**

The negotiation had begun!

Samson gave the men this riddle:

> Out of the eater came forth meat, and out of the
> strong came forth sweetness.

> **Judges 14:14**

For three days, the men tried to answer the riddle
but could not. Then the men said to Samson's bride,

> Entice thy husband, that he may declare unto
> us the riddle, lest we burn thee and thy father's
> house with fire: have ye called us to take that
> we have? is it not so?

> **Judges 14:15**

So Samson's wife wept before Samson and said,

> Thou dost but hate me, and lovest me not: thou
> hast put forth a riddle unto the children of my
> people, and hast not told it me. And he said
> unto her, Behold, I have not told it my father
> nor my mother, and shall I tell it thee?

> **Judges 14:16**

At this, his wife wept all the more — in fact, she
wept for the remainder of the seven-day wedding
feast. Finally, her tears wore him down and he told
her the answer to the riddle. By the time the sun
went down on the seventh day, the men gave
Samson the correct answer. Samson was furious.

He knew the only way they could have come up with the right answer was to get the answer from his wife. He said, **If ye had not plowed with my heifer, ye had not found out my riddle** (Judges 14:18).

Then Samson proceeded to tear the place apart. The Bible says **the Spirit of the Lord came upon him** (Judges 14:19). Samson went down to Ashkelon, another Philistine city, and there he killed thirty men. He took their garments and gave them to the thirty men who had solved the riddle, which was the debt he owed to them. Still angry, Samson went back to his parents' house.

Can you see the pattern in Samson's life? He gets involved with a Philistine girl — an ungodly woman who is his enemy. He goes against the wishes of his parents, which in a broader sense is going against the wishes of God. And he begins to play games with his enemy. The pattern is fully established — it is no different than the pattern of his behavior with Delilah years later.

The story of the woman from Timnath didn't end there, however. After Samson had cooled off, he went back to see his wife, but her father prohibited him from going into her bedchamber. He said to Samson,

> **I verily thought that thou hadst utterly hated her; therefore I gave her to thy companion: is not her younger sister fairer than she? take her, I pray thee, instead of her.**
>
> **Judges 15:2**

Samson's wife had married one of Samson's best friends. Talk about anger! Samson really let loose. He caught three hundred foxes, which takes not only some skill but some strength and courage, tied their tails together with firebrands in between each two foxes, and then set those animals out into the standing corn fields of the Philistines, burning up not only their shocks and standing corn, but also the neighboring vineyards and olive groves. (See Judges 15:4,5.) When they saw what had happened and discovered the reason for Samson's action, the Philistines killed the girl and her father *by burning them.* It was a tragedy all around. One act of treachery led to another and then to another.

That's what happens when we get into bad patterns in our lives, and we don't face up to them and turn to God for help in changing our ways. We set into motion one tragedy after another, one mistake after another, one sin after another. Our initial sin never ends with us, and it doesn't end in us — unless we confess that sin fully, ask for and receive God's forgiveness, and by the power of the Holy Spirit and strength of God's Word, change the pattern of our behavior.

It's one thing for us to say that a man has sinned. That's going to be true of every man or woman who ever enters into a relationship. Every woman marries a man who has sinned. Every man marries a woman who has sinned — in some way, at some time, with some person.

What matters far more than the fact that a person has sinned is this: What did that person do about that sin? Did they try to deny it? Ignore it? Let it go unrepented and unchanged?

Has the *pattern of sin* taken root in the person's life or was that pattern of sin changed?

In Samson's case, the pattern that was started with the girl from Timnath wasn't changed. It lay dormant for years, and then it repeated itself in Samson's relationship with Delilah — to Samson's great loss!

To say that every person has sinned in some way does not necessarily mean that the person has sinned sexually. The sin may have been drinking, using drugs, spending money on gambling, or engaging in other vices. It may have been a pattern of lying and cheating — in school, and then in the workplace. It may have been a pattern of abuse — of venting one's anger in unhealthy, destructive ways.

AVOID DANGEROUS GAMES

The negotiation of Samson with the men who came to his wedding feast was not the only negotiation in which Samson participated. On one occasion, the men of Judah came to him at his home in Etam and said, **We are come down to bind thee, that we may deliver thee into the hand of the Philistines** (Judges 15:12). They intended to turn him over to the Philistines in exchange for peace.

Samson went along with their plan. He said to them, **Swear unto me, that ye will not fall upon me yourselves.** They agreed, saying, **We will bind thee fast, and deliver thee into their hand: but surely we will not kill thee** (Judges 15:12,13). Then they bound him with two new cords and brought him to the Philistines.

When the Philistines began to shout against the captive Samson, however, the Spirit of the Lord came upon Samson and the cords that were on his arms **became as flax that was burnt with fire, and his bands loosed from off his hands** (Judges 15:14). Samson went after the men with a vengeance and killed a thousand of them before he was through.

Can you see the pattern here? Samson allows himself to be bound. He frees himself and defeats the enemy. We see it in Delilah all over again.

One thing we see about Samson in the Bible is that he was not only a man of great strength, but that he tended to display that strength in ways that were "out of control" time after time after time. It may be a very normal response to the roar of a lion that is attacking your life to kill that lion, even to tear it limb from limb. It is not, however, a normal response for a man to take three hundred foxes — which may actually have been jackals, very dangerous animals — and tie their tails together and put firebrands in each knot and set those animals afire into Philistine fields, vineyards, and orchards! Samson's anger was out of control!

After Samson's wife and father-in-law were killed, he went on yet another killing spree. The Bible says he **smote them hip and thigh with a great slaughter** (Judges 15:8). At another time, Samson killed a thousand men with the fresh jawbone of a dead donkey. (See Judges 15:15,16.) There's a pattern of uncontrolled anger in Samson's life.

Countless men are wound up very tight today. Push them too hard and you set them off. They are time bombs of old patterns just waiting to explode. Watch them. Stand back.

Deal With Pressure — or You'll Explode. Many men go to great lengths to cover the pressure they feel. And who can say that our world isn't filled with pressure? There's pressure to pay the bills, pressure to succeed in your chosen job, pressure to take responsibility for your life and the lives of your spouse and children, pressure to live up to the neighbor's expectations, pressure to put on a good face at church.

Deep down inside, pressure builds up and begins to eat away at a person's core. If a person doesn't deal with the pressure and release it in healthy and godly ways, pressure will build up...and up...and up...until the lid blows, just like a pressure cooker when the pressure gets too high.

One of the most effective ways of dealing with pressure is to admit that you are feeling pressure and to talk about it. Men often talk about anything but the pressure they feel inside. They'll talk about sports. They'll talk about their jobs. They'll talk about the "times" and how tough things are. But they rarely talk about how they are feeling or the stress and pressure they feel inside. If we don't admit to the pressure and talk about it, it builds. And builds. And builds. Then it's not a matter of if there will be an explosion, but *when* the explosion will occur.

Make Decisions That "Lower the Temperature." Many men in jail today are not inherently bad, but they got themselves into a position of pain and pressure, and they didn't know how to express that pain or release that pressure. They are victims of the devil, who was out to get them from their birth.

Samson was not an inherently bad man. The exact opposite was true — from his birth he had a divine call on his life to be a strong emancipator of his people. But Samson got caught up in a "position" that wasn't good. He became the victim of that position in which he had put himself. That's no excuse for Samson — he should have known enough to keep himself out of that position. Nevertheless, it's the reality of the situation. Samson painted himself into a corner with his decisions.

Expose the Myth of "Self-Management." How many times do we hear ourselves say, "I can manage it by myself. I can handle it." The fact is, if we are under such a load of trouble or experiencing such a high degree of pressure that we have to make such a statement — then we *can't* handle the problem ourselves. In reality, the problem is managing us far more than we are capable of managing the problem. The moment something upsets our balance or we run into enemy territory and take a hit, we lose all ability to manage the problem. Things go out of control.

One of the reasons we think we can handle the problem is that the world tells us we can handle it. The media *tells* us in a thousand ways every day that we can take control of our own lives and our own destiny. But very few people have any real-life examples of people who have either taken control of their own lives successfully or who have turned over control of their lives to God — which is the only genuine, successful management of any problem.

Most men don't have a godly man as their role model. They didn't grow up with one and they don't have one in their life now. In many cases, men in the Church didn't grow up with a godly man as a role model either. They don't have a clue as to how to turn their problems over to God and avail themselves of His assistance in the management of their problems. They only have the media version of the "macho man" who is in control of his own destiny through means of power. They see Shaft or Rambo or the Terminator as someone who has *control*.

The result of this mentality of self-management is this: Most men reach manhood and try to manage life solely on the basis of trial and error experimentation. Along the way, men make a lot of mistakes. In the wake of a lack of teaching in the laboratory of manhood, young men sometimes make *a whole lot of mistakes!*

They emerge from their own self-governed laboratories covered with the dust and soot of their own explosions, still trying to present to the public a facade of success. Inside, men know they have made mistakes and experienced failure. But their pride forces them to say, "It was no big deal. So I didn't handle it well. Next time I will." But next time, the pattern continues — different faces, different situations, different methods, but the same disastrous results.

A deadly cycle or pattern begins. The person eventually becomes so numb to their own silent pain that they don't even know they hurt. If they aren't hurting, they make no effort to remedy the source of their pain. If there's no effort to fix what has gone wrong, there's going to be a repeat of old behavior.

DIFFUSING THE TIME BOMB

A man who has shut himself down regarding his own sinful patterns of behavior is a person who is ripe for Delilah to come walking into his life. But this pattern of repeating behavior isn't only true for men with anger, of course. It relates to all damaging patterns of the past and is true for women too. Furthermore, destructive behavior patterns are often repeated not only within one person's life, but from generation to generation.

One of the damaging patterns that occurs in many marriages is a lingering memory of past abuse. In the movie, *Forrest Gump,* the character of Jenny goes through her short life experimenting with drugs, sex, and other efforts to "find herself" in the aftermath of an abusive childhood. Many people are like Jenny. They are struggling with negative seeds that were sown early in their lives. In virtually all cases, we can point to those negative seeds and identify their origin: The parents were not living in the order established by God. It's very difficult for an adult to parent children if they are the product of bad parenting.

Many people live in bondage today because of things that occurred in their childhood homes. Even as adults they are trying to work through the hang-ups, the lack of love and encouragement, and the failures they experienced as children.

We must recognize that the flaws of our childhood act as "time bombs" within us. Very often they show up just a little while after we say "I do" to a husband or a wife.

It is so important that we come to the Lord as *single* people, before we enter into marriage, and pray, "Search me, O God, and if You find anything in me that is not clean or not right, I ask You to bring it to light so that I might confess it, be forgiven for it, repent of it, and begin to rely on You for a transformation in my life."

Before you say "I do" is the best time for you to get rid of the hang-ups that might be time bombs to destroy your marriage.

But for those of you who are married and are struggling with these "explosions" in your home, it's not too late. There's still an opportunity for you and your spouse to come to God in the same way and seek His forgiveness and His healing and His help in starting over anew in your relationship.

With God's help, you can defuse the time bombs that have been set to go off in your life and in your marriage!

Take an Honest Inventory of Yourself. If you have had a repeated problem over the years — a problem that just seems to reoccur and reoccur — then ask yourself, "What is it that the devil knows about me that I don't know about myself?" Somewhere in your life there's a door that's been left open to the devil. It may be something you thought you had dealt with, or that has its root so long ago that you have forgotten it. Ask the Holy Spirit to bring that thing to your mind so you can deal with it and receive God's help with it.

Take an honest inventory of what you are on the inside. Are you a giving person? Are you a truthful person? Are you a person who is going to make a decision and stick with it? Are you a person who wants what God wants rather than what you want?

Ask yourself, "What's in me? What motivates me? What drives me? What causes me to do the things I do?"

You can't expect a spouse to understand you if you don't understand yourself. When your spouse asks you, "What's going on in you?" and you don't have an answer, how on earth is your spouse supposed to minister to you, help you, comfort you, or even pray for you?

Don't Live in Denial About Old Patterns. Not only must we face up to the old patterns in our own lives, but also in the life of the man or woman we are considering as a marriage partner. What pattern is there in that person's life? What sin seems to manifest itself again and again? And more importantly, what is the person doing about that sin? Are they repenting before God? Are they asking for God's help in abstaining from that sin and changing their ways? Is the pattern being broken by the power of God?

Old patterns don't fade away with time — they just go underground. Old patterns don't die. They remain latent in a person, just waiting to be triggered into action. An old pattern will not disappear over time. It merely will go dormant, only to erupt later. Unless a pattern is brought to the healing and delivering power of Jesus Christ, it *will resurface,* and usually when you least expect it.

The Bible has a number of examples of people who repeated patterns of behavior that went unrepented and unchanged. For example:

• Saul continued to pursue David, even after he had said he would not harm him.

• Jezebel continued to pursue Elijah, even after powerful miracle manifestations.

• Herod continued to be a skeptic and an unrighteous man even though he was "sad" at the beheading of John the Baptist, the man who had criticized him.

Simply to face one's track record of sinful behavior isn't enough. One must confess that this behavior is wrong before God, ask for and receive God's forgiveness, and then repent — which is to change one's ways. The Holy Spirit is our gift from God to help us change. Our reliance upon Him must be daily.

I recently lost some weight I had been carrying for a long time. For years I had a desire to lose weight. I knew that I *should* lose some weight, but I never really knew just how overweight I was because I refused to get on a scale. I didn't want to know what I weighed. I set out to try to lose weight to the point where I was comfortable getting on the scale to see what I actually did weigh!

Now I know that may sound a little crazy to you, but that was how I felt. I just didn't have the nerve to face up to what I actually weighed. Had I stared at those cold, hard numbers on the scale a little earlier, I may very well have become more serious about my diet a little earlier!

Don't put your head into the sand about what is wrong in your life or in your marriage. Face up to it. Just having a desire to see your marriage improved isn't enough. Even acknowledging that your marriage should be different before God isn't enough. You have to face the reality of what is wrong so you know just what needs to be changed, fixed, or repaired.

God will not help you to fix the mess your marriage is in until you have faced the mess, acknowledged that it *is* a mess, and come to an understanding about precisely what it is that needs to be changed, healed, or repaired.

You must own up to the mistakes that were made in your life, which *you* have made. Face them. Don't deny them, try to justify them, or sweep them under some kind of emotional rug. Face them. Then take them to God and say, "Here is what is wrong in my life. Please forgive me. Please fix me! Help me not to carry on this pattern. Emancipate me from the devil's hold on my life and on the curse that the devil has put there in the past. Free me! And help me to walk into my future according to Your plan and purpose."

Don't hide from your past problems.

Don't run from them.

Don't ignore them.

Deal with them, with God's help. You were born to solve these problems!

Remember: No Problem Is Too Hard for God. The good news is that there isn't a repeated behavioral pattern that's too difficult for God to change.

There isn't a question that is beyond His ability to answer.

There isn't a need He can't meet.

There isn't a pain He can't heal.

There isn't anything broken He can't fix.

Don't limp and drag yourself along through life because of what happened to you when you were a child. Don't allow the attitudes and prejudices and environment of your early years dictate to you what you will become in your future. Don't allow an old poverty syndrome or a low self-esteem syndrome become the norm for your life.

God has something better for you! He has a new reality for you.

Your past does not need to be your present or your future!

Believe That Change Is Possible. Can behavior change? Absolutely. We find a number of examples throughout the Bible:

• Abraham didn't father children by other women after his experience with Hagar.

• Moses didn't kill anyone else after he had killed an abusive Egyptian and escaped to the deserts of Midian.

• David didn't sin with another woman after Bathsheba and his repentance in the presence of the prophet Nathan.

• Paul didn't persecute Christians after his Damascus road experience.

Change is possible when one turns to God and trusts Him completely for help in making a positive change.

If you will engage in the battle against Satan for your marriage and your family, you will win that battle. There isn't a spiritual battle that you haven't already "won" in Christ Jesus. You just need to move in and claim your victory.

If you will face up to what it is that you need to do to get your marriage and your relationship with your children back on track, God will help you do that which you know to do and are committed to doing. He will help you win the war for your family by breaking every destructive pattern in your lives!

CHAPTER 11

COMING BACK TO OUR FUTURE

I f there ever was a man who needed a true woman of God to help him through the challenges he faced and to provide for him a place, a sanctuary, and honor, it was Samson. Delilah was *not* that woman. She failed him miserably.

If there ever was a man who needed a strong father to train him in the ways of the Lord, it was Samson. His father, unfortunately, also failed him badly.

Samson went down to Timnath and saw a Philistine woman that caught his eye and captured his fancy. He came home and said to his father, **Get her for me to wife** (Judges 14:2). In effect he was saying, "I want to marry an enemy girl. I want to align myself with the people God has told me to defeat. Make the arrangements for me." And the sad news in this story is that Samson's father did what Samson asked!

To the credit of Manoah, Samson's father, he tried to warn Samson about the woman from Timnath. He said, along with Samson's mother, **Is there never a woman among the daughters of**

thy brethren, or among all my people, that thou goest to take a wife of the uncircumcised Philistines? (Judges 14:3). But Samson wouldn't hear any of it. He said again to his father, **Get her for me; for she pleaseth me well** (Judges 14:3).

We should never be surprised when worldly people are unmoved even after their attention has been called to the fact that they are about to commit a sin or err in the sight of God. Those who are in the world have a job description of sin. Sin is what sinners do. Sinners don't mind wallowing around in sin. Until they are brought to the point of conviction, they are very comfortable in their sin and have no desire to change.

But when saints sin, they have misread their job description, which is to do the works of Jesus. A true saint will want to repent of their sin and be cleansed of it. They won't want to linger in it. One of the best ways you can know if a person is a genuine Christian is to see how they respond if sin is brought to their attention. The genuine Christian will own up to sin and seek forgiveness of it.

> **Love not the world, neither the things that are in the world. If any man love the world, the love of the Father is not in him.**
>
> **For all that is in the world, the lust of the flesh, and the lust of the eyes, and the pride of life, is not of the Father, but is of the world.**
>
> **1 John 2:15,16**

Samson's refusal to heed the words of his father should have been a clear sign to Manoah and to Mrs. Manoah that they hadn't fully trained up Samson in the ways of the Lord. The fact that Samson still wanted an uncircumcised Philistine girl even after they had warned him of the danger was a sure sign he did not have the wisdom of God operating in him. He had the strength and power of God; he had a mandate from God, but Samson did not have the wisdom of God. He was operating totally on the lust of the eyes.

John concluded his statement about loving the world this way:

> **And the world passeth away, and the lust thereof: but he that doeth the will of God abideth for ever.**
>
> **1 John 2:17**

We must teach our children from an early age that the will of God is the most important thing they can discern, know, understand, and follow. If they follow only their own fleshly lusts — what they see, what they feel, what they want out of pride — they are going to end up in a sad, sad state.

WHAT DOES IT MEAN TO "TRAIN UP"?

Proverbs 22:6 is a verse that many parents know: **Train up a child in the way he should go: and when he is old, he will not depart from it.** What does "train up" really mean?

To "train" means far more than teaching your child a few Bible verses and taking them to church every Sunday. That's part of it, but that's not the whole story. To train up is a whole-life experience. It's *insisting* that your child go in the right way until they are an adult and are no longer in your home.

I liken this to a train moving down a track. The engine is the only part of the train that has power. Parents are the engine in a family. They empower the rest of the train. All of the cars are hooked to the engine and they just follow wherever the engine goes. They have no choice, no option, no decision-making power.

So many parents today ask their children if they want to go to church or if they want to go to church camp or to Sunday school. It's not the child's choice to make! It's the parent's choice. The same for teenagers. As long as parents have responsibility for a child in their home, they have authority over that child.

Other parents allow a child to choose which religion they want to follow. I've even heard parents say, "I'm not taking my child to church because I want him to be able to make up his own mind when he's an adult." The fact is, such a parent is already making up that child's mind for him now! He's making up his mind *not* to go to *any* church.

In Samson's case, he was under his father's authority until he married the woman that his father arranged for him to marry. But Samson's father didn't take full responsibility for his son and exercise the rightful authority he had.

When Samson came home and said, "Listen, Dad, I want to marry a woman that's outside my faith and outside my people — in fact, she's even one of the enemy — but I like the way she looks so get her for me," Samson's father should have said, "You're my son and I love you, but I'm not getting you what you think you want. This woman is wrong for you and here's why. I'm not going to be a party in this marriage." That may sound tough to you, but it would have been the right thing to do, and the rest of Samson's story bears that out.

There was a time in our culture when what was taught to you in the home was the same as what was expected of you at the school, and that was the same as what was expected in the community. If I got a whipping at home for something, I got that same whipping at school for doing the same thing, and I would get a whipping in the neighborhood from an adult who caught me doing the same thing. I had no recourse. I didn't talk back. I didn't fight back. That was the way things were. I was hedged in on all corners. And it was for my good.

Today children are in a different situation. The school and the community may teach or allow things that are very different from what is being taught or allowed in the home. It's even *more* important, therefore, that parents stand firm.

A parent is the number one influence on a child. And that influence needs to be firm, and stand for what God says.

Don't Let Children Make Adult Decisions. My mom always said to me, "Be home before dark." The reason she told me that was because I didn't have enough sense to know what could happen in the dark! It was a long time before I was wise enough to choose between right and wrong, and between what was foolish and what was wise behavior.

Don't allow your children to make adult decisions they don't have the information they need to make a smart choice. They need wisdom, and wisdom takes time and experience. You can't just say to your child, "Dope is bad, so don't do drugs," then turn your child out onto the street at all hours of the day and night and expect them not to get hooked into the wrong crowd and experiment with drugs. The same goes for anything else that has the potential to destroy your child's life and wound his spirit.

Take Authority Over Your Child's Friendships and Know Where Your Child Goes. It isn't up to the child to decide when they get up or how late they stay out or who their friends will be or what parties they will go to or how they will spend their time. That's the parents' responsibility. And as long as a parent has responsibility, a parent has authority.

As a child, there were lots of places I wasn't allowed to go. In raising my children, there were lots of places I haven't allowed my sons to spend the night. I didn't know those other parents. I didn't know what would be allowed in their homes. And until I knew with a certainty that my sons were not going to be harmed in any way, I wasn't about to allow my sons to go for an overnight visit.

When I was in junior high school, there was a guy who became my buddy. I liked him, but my mamma didn't. She *killed* my friendship with that guy. She saw something in him that she knew was wrong and she had a strong opinion that if I continued on in my friendship with this boy, I'd end up in hell.

Now I didn't have enough sense to see what Mamma saw. I was totally caught up in the fun and craziness of being with that buddy of mine. He was my ace. When I look back now, I know Mamma was right. I'm grateful for what she did. But at the time, I couldn't see it. And neither can your child see with wisdom who their friends should be. They can't determine with wisdom where they should go or what they should expose themselves to.

Samson went to Timnath. This was a city on the edge of Philistia. He had no business going to that neighborhood! His father should have, and could have, stopped him.

How Long Do You Have Authority Over Your Child?

For a number of years I told my sons, "When you turn eighteen, I'll help you pack. You're out of here." But then the Lord convicted me about this.

He reminded me of His Word: **For this cause shall a man leave his father and mother, and shall be joined unto his wife** (Ephesians 5:31). I saw that I am responsible for my son until he is mature enough to leave my home and start another home with a wife. Until then, he's my responsibility. It's my job to help him become mature and to find the right woman. It's my job to tell him, "You're ready now. It's time you take a wife."

Lots of boys are marrying women today. Are you aware that about 32 percent of all single males between the ages of 25 and 34 still live at home? Only about 20 percent of women in that age range are at home.

Leaving home is not just a physical act. It's a mental and emotional act. It means you no longer look to your parents to provide for you, cover for you, make decisions for you, support you, solve problems for you. Neither are you reliant upon their spiritual covering of you as a child.

The purpose of leaving home is not to place that burden upon a wife. Lots of men are looking for their wives to be their mothers — to nurture them as Mamma did, to provide for them, and even to support them financially. When a man decides to marry, he must be 100 percent certain that he is willing to leave his parents and start a new home with the maturity and the resources in place to make that home a place in which a wife can be nurtured and protected, and children can be born and thrive.

Any issues of childhood need to be left behind, resolved, and dealt with before God. A father must help his son and his daughter deal with those issues before the child leaves home. Until a man is ready to assume full responsibility for protecting and providing for a wife and children, he has no business getting married. Until a woman knows what it means to be a helpmate to a man and is prepared to do so, she has no business getting married.

Do Not Leave in Rebellion. Leaving parents and cleaving to a spouse was never intended to be an act of rebellion against parents. There are many young men — still boys in their emotional makeup — who think, *If I can just get away from my parents, I'll be a man.* Young women sometimes think that way too. No! Become a man or woman of God and then leave your parents and marry. If you leave your parents in a spirit of rebellion, you are going into any new relationship you establish with that spirit of rebellion boiling inside you. It will poison everything you try to do.

Deal with your childhood issues before you leave home. Come to grips with your life before you involve someone else in it.

As an Adult, Stop Blaming Your Parents. Even though your parents may have failed you, once you are an adult, you have no privilege before God to blame your parents for your failures. Did Samson *have* to fall into sin and a wrong pattern because his father failed him? No! Samson could have repented. He could have stood strong in his own right.

There is no "my parents ruined me" excuse that is acceptable to God. Just as you can't say, "The devil made me do it," and get away with that excuse before God, neither can you say, "I'm a victim of my upbringing. My father and mother made me do it." They may have set a bad example for you, but they are not responsible for *your choosing* to reject God's plan and live according to your own plan. They may not have done everything right, but they are not responsible for what you have the power to choose to do once you are an adult!

CHOOSING A SPOUSE

One of the most important roles you have as a parent is to help your child choose a spouse with wisdom and according to God's normal progression for a godly relationship.

Do you remember the story of Abraham and Isaac? When Abraham was old, he sent the oldest servant in his house back to his people and said, **Take a wife unto my son Isaac.** (See Genesis 24:1-4.) Isaac may have been almost forty years old by this time! Sarah was 90 years old when Isaac was born and she died at the age of 127. It was well after the period of mourning for Sarah that Abraham started planning for a wife for Isaac. Isaac was *at least* 37 years old when Abraham was choosing a wife for him.

The fact is, Abraham knew this was his responsibility and he had the prevailing belief, "My son isn't responsible for this choice. I am. My boy is not about to marry a Canaanite woman who worships false gods. If he marries that kind of woman, he'll be unequally yoked. He needs a woman who will support his belief in the one, true, and living God and who will worship God like I've trained him up to worship Him. Then even after I am dead, he'll carry on the faith."

Help your child find a spouse who is a strong Christian. I'm not talking about someone who just says "I'm saved," but someone who is walking the Christian walk and understanding the plan and purposes of God for this generation. Find someone who is truly following Jesus as Lord and Master and who desires most of all to obey God's plan for marriage.

It doesn't matter if your child comes home and says, "But I'm in love. I feel things in my heart for this person." That's precisely what Samson said. The heart generally doesn't know what it wants, and it most certainly doesn't know what it *needs*. A parent has much greater objectivity and should have much greater wisdom. Activate that wisdom on behalf of your child!

Train Up an Heir to Follow You in the Faith. Don't fail your child in helping them choose a mate. If you fail your child, you are also failing your as-yet-unborn grandchildren, and in turn, even your future great grandchildren.

We have clear examples of this kind of failure in the Bible. King David failed miserably as a father. He didn't discipline his children. He didn't punish them when they did wrong, even when one of his sons raped one of his daughters! He didn't put a stop to Absalom's rebellion. And he had problems with his sons.

Along came Solomon and he too failed as a father. Two of the saddest verses in all the Bible are Ecclesiastes 2:18,19:

> **Yea, I hated all my labour which I had taken under the sun: because I should leave it unto the man that shall be after me.**
> **And who knoweth whether he shall be a wise man or a fool?**

Solomon is lamenting the fact that he has become the first billionaire in the history of the world and he doesn't have a child worthy of turning the kingdom over to. He doesn't know who his sons are or whether they are wise or foolish! Why doesn't he know? He should know. He's their father!

It was because of Solomon's failure as a father that his children subsequently divided the kingdom that David had built and Solomon had strengthened. When the kingdom became divided, it became weak and it fell apart. The generations repeated themselves in failure. They missed out on

God's perfect plan because "good ol' Dad" didn't stand up and demand what was right before God.

Train up your child how to read and understand God's Word.

Train up your child how to handle wealth — how to work, earn, save, invest, and spend wisely.

Train up your child how to praise God and to worship Him in service, time, talent, and resources.

Train up your child how to treat other people, including how to treat you and your spouse, so they will one day know how to treat their own spouse and children.

Train up your child to respect the authority of those in leadership in their church and in their community.

Train up your child!

Do what is right, be the role model, be the engine that drives their train down the right track of life!

MY EXHORTATION TO FATHERS

A father's responsibility is to teach his children the works and commandments of God and to show by his example how to obey the commandments of God and to praise God for His blessings. In other words, a father's responsibility is to teach his child right from wrong. If a father doesn't do that for his children, they will be children without hope and without a solid foundation for their lives. They will be a stubborn and rebellious generation.

In the absence of a father fulfilling this role for his children, the responsibility falls to the child's pastor to teach the children these very things — the commandments of God and how to keep them, and how to praise God for His strength and the wonderful works He has done on their behalf.

A boy came up to me one Sunday and said, "I had a conversation with my mother and I told her that since my daddy isn't at home, I'm taking you as my daddy. And my mother said, 'That isn't right, your daddy is so-and-so.'"

I said to this young man, "No, you were right. I'm your daddy in the spirit." And that is what a pastor is if a child doesn't have a father in the home. The pastor becomes the spiritual covering for that child. He will receive his spiritual instruction about the Word of God from me.

To fail to give a child a genuine understanding of right and wrong is to raise a child who is angry — at himself, at the world, at life in general.

Much of what I say and do today is my daddy talking. I know that. I have studied and I continue to study. I have a master's degree in divinity. I have read the Word and I preach the Word. But there are times when I hear myself preaching and I think to myself, *That's Daddy talking.* Something my father said — at a time and place I can't even recall — took root in me and grew and now it comes out of me. That's true for you and your children. They won't even know all that they are learning from you until they hear it come out of their own mouths one day.

You are the engine that powers not only their behavior, but their thinking, their values, their beliefs, and their opinions. The Holy Ghost brings back what has been deposited in a person about Jesus and about God's truth. There's a transference in the spirit that goes from father to child, from pastor to the person in the pew, from generation to generation.

Lay your hands on your sons and daughters and tell them who they are before God and who they are in your own heart. Plant into them the seeds that God will grow and turn into a harvest of good on their behalf.

How to Lose Everything That Truly Matters. Consider the story of Eli in the Bible. Here was a man who was chosen to be the high priest of the Israelites. He was considered the most spiritual man in all the nation. Eli had a great influence upon young Samuel, who would become a high priest and prophet later in his life. But Eli missed doing the most important job that had been given to him: He failed to discipline his sons in the Lord. Eli was judged severely.

> **I will judge his house for ever for the iniquity which he knoweth; because his sons made themselves vile, and he restrained them not.**
>
> **1 Samuel 3:13**

The Bible says that Eli knew he wasn't doing the right thing and that the judgment of God was facing him, yet he still failed to act as he should have acted! Eli's sons were not keeping the proper customs related to the sacrifices that the people brought to God. Furthermore, the Bible tells us that they **lay with the women that assembled at the door of the tabernacle of the congregation** (1 Samuel 2:22).

Eli had confronted his sons with their errors and had told them the truth, but he had not *insisted* that they change their ways. It should have been a matter of, "You change or you're no longer to function as a priest." Eli didn't demand that, and God judged him for it. He saw his sons killed and the ark of the covenant taken away by the enemy. In the end, the shock of all that he had lost caused him to fall and break his neck. That was a heavy price to pay for failing to do the right thing as a father!

You can lose everything you have, and everything your children might one day gain, if you fail to discipline your children in the Lord and to *insist* that they follow the ways of the Lord while they are under your authority and you have responsibility for them.

Lead Your Child All the Way to the Cross of Christ. If you are going to witness to only one person on this earth, make sure that person is your child. As a parent, your children *are* your foremost mission field. You have a responsibility before God to make certain that your child knows how to accept Jesus Christ as their personal Savior, and that they have a *desire* to be saved.

Let me give you an illustration of the authority that a father has over his children in leading them to Christ. One Saturday night my father came into the room where my brothers and I were. He said, "Boys, tomorrow when I preach" — he was an associate pastor at the time and he had been scheduled to preach that particular Sunday — "all four of you boys are going to get saved. All four of you are getting saved *tomorrow*." I was saved under a mandate from my dad! My three brothers and I were all saved in one day. We had a mandate from our father to accept Jesus Christ.

My brothers and I were not convicted on the basis of what my father preached. We were convicted on the basis of the way he looked at us and spoke to us on Saturday night. He was basing his statement to us on the Word of God: **As for me and my house, we will serve the Lord** (Joshua 24:15).

That following Sunday morning, as soon as my father finished preaching and extended the invitation for people to get saved, all four of us got up and walked in line down the aisle. People were shouting hallelujahs that morning. They didn't know we were under a mandate.

Now, if my father had sat down and explained to us a little more about what was going on and what our decision really meant, we might have *really* been saved that morning, but he didn't do that.

Even so, we all finally came to that point. That Sunday morning of our "getting saved" was like a dress rehearsal of things to come. I honor my father on this point: He wasn't about to let us go astray. He was determined to make sure that his boys were right with God.

Do you have that same determination for your child? Are you that committed to your child coming to know the Lord that you will insist on it? Insist in the spirit realm. Let the devil know that he has no ownership over your child. Explain the full meaning of salvation to your child. Lead them — train them up — to that decision in their life.

A Father's Mandate From God. I believe the first thing God is going to ask fathers when they get to heaven is, "Where's your children?" You will be asked to give an account for how you have trained up your children. It is *your* responsibility, not the responsibility of your wife. You are called by God to be a priest, prophet, protector, and covering for your child.

Priest. You are called to bring your children to God. That's what a priest does — he brings the people before God.

Prophet. You are called to declare the Word of God to your children. That is what a prophet does — he declares God's Word.

Protector. You are called to defend, provide, and preserve your children. In a practical way, you must feed, clothe, and house your children so they grow up with their basic needs met and they experience the best health and well-being possible.

Cover. You are to be the spiritual cover for your children, and that means you engage in whatever spiritual warfare is necessary for them to grow up emotionally and spiritually strong before God. God will *not* let you off the hook about this! God is not only concerned about you and your children, but about the *next* generation to come. He's building for Himself a people, a lineage, an inheritance.

When the husband is out of place spiritually, then God will rest that anointing upon the mother. Even so, she should pray for godly men to "father" her children in the Lord, to fill that void in them that needs a man. I'm not saying she should go out and marry the first church-going man she finds! I am saying she should pray for godly men — relatives, pastors, teachers, coaches, Sunday school teachers, and youth leaders — to fill that gap in her children's lives.

THE IMPORTANCE OF TRAINING THE NEXT GENERATION

All true "wealth" — which is largely those things money cannot buy — is passed on through the family. It goes from generation to generation. *You are a patriarch or a matriarch not only over your immediate family, but over all those who will be your heirs!*

In any area of life, you'll find this principle to be true. Spiritual wealth moves from believer to believer, generation to generation. Those with godly parents have a much greater likelihood of leading godly lives. It's true for physical and emotional health, for a good ability to relate to others in a positive and healthy way, for a knowledge of the Word of God, for commitment to the church, for intellectual ability and common sense, for cultural and religious values. Show me the parents, I'll predict for you the children. Exceptions always exist, but for the most part, the true wealth of our lives is passed from father to son, mother to daughter.

The great fortunes of the world are also passed from parents to children, but monetary fortunes can be lost much more readily than the "inner" wealth that belongs to us as God's children. The family is God's vehicle for "passing on" what is of the greatest value.

What will save and enrich the world of tomorrow is what saves and enriches the world today — the Gospel of Jesus Christ and strong families who will carry God's principles from one generation to the next. What we do in our marriages and in our families is what will *be* the world of tomorrow.

The sad fact for many people, however, is that they do not have godly role models. We live in a culture where countless adults did not have the right things passed on to them from the previous generation. They don't know how to live godly lives because they didn't have anyone to model godly lives for them. The result is that we are off course from God's plan. If we continue in this direction, we are headed for major head-on collisions that will be 100 percent fatal.

God's Word tells us plainly,

> **Be not deceived; God is not mocked: for whatsoever a man soweth, that shall he also reap.**
>
> **For he that soweth to his flesh shall of the flesh reap corruption; but he that soweth to the Spirit shall of the Spirit reap life everlasting.**
>
> **Galatians 6:7,8**

We face an uphill battle, a serious struggle, because we have to overcome years — in some cases, generations — of both ignorance about and disobedience to God's Word.

Paul had a serious struggle in his day, but I believe our struggle is even greater today. Paul didn't have HBO, Cinemax, and the Playboy channel piped into every home. Paul didn't have to see naked bodies every time he went to the movies, or see liquor on every billboard he passed by. He didn't have to walk down streets where someone was trying to sell drugs on every corner.

If you went into most public schools today and had an opportunity to talk openly about Jesus and the Holy Spirit, most of the children in those schools would look at you as if you were speaking a foreign language. They don't even know what they don't know!

Even the slang terminology of our culture is working against us. I recently went into a barbershop and a man greeted another man as he came through the door, "Hey, dog!" Dog? I refuse to receive that. I know what a dog is and how a dog acts and I don't have any desire whatsoever to be a dog. If we call one another dogs long enough, we'll start thinking that's our job description.

Every generation is only one generation from failure. If you fail your child, you have failed the next generation that follows your child. In some cases, we have communities that have lived in failure for generation after generation. Samson's father erred greatly in the way he handled Samson's marriage, but the reason for his father's failure runs deep. In Judges 2:10 we read:

> **And also all that generation were gathered unto their fathers: and there arose another generation after them, which knew not the Lord, nor yet the works which he had done for Israel.**

Deborah and Barak, and then Gideon, served as judges over Israel before we get to the story of Samson. So were people named Tola and Jair and Jephthah. During each judge's reign the Israelites were delivered for a period of time, and then they fell back into old, evil patterns. At the time Samson was born, this was the situation:

> **And the children of Israel did evil again in the sight of the Lord; and the Lord delivered them into the hand of the Philistines forty years.**
>
> **Judges 13:1**

By the time Samson was born, there had been at least one full generation of "evil doing," of separation from the ways of the Lord. By the time Samson was old enough to marry, the people had been living for at least sixty years under Philistine rule.

It takes a strong person to swim against that kind of tide and to turn things back to righteousness. It would have taken a strong father to say no to Samson. The task would not have been impossible, but it would have taken great inner strength and courage. Manoah didn't have that strength of conviction, even though an angel had told him how to raise Samson. Although he had raised his son to be a Nazarite — no wine or strong drink, no unclean foods, no razor touching his head — he had not raised his son in *all* the ways of the Lord.

The challenge we face today is no less than the challenge Samson's father faced. Our children are growing up in a mostly unrighteous, ungodly society. We must have *great* strength if we are to stand against the evil tide that wants to destroy our children. Furthermore, our nation is living under a curse. You only have to take a look at the abortion rate, the divorce rate, the domestic violence rate, the crime rate, and the interest rates to know that we rate an "F" for failure as a society.

It's up to God's people to bring our nation back into a blessing. And the only way that will happen is the way it happened throughout the Bible — through repentance and forgiveness and a determination to move forward in what is right before God. It will take *great* strength and courage — but look at what is at stake.

Look what happened to Samson because his daddy didn't stand up and say, "No, son. This woman isn't right for you. I'm going to find a godly woman for you." Not only was Samson destroyed emotionally and physically by Delilah, but it was years and years before Samson fulfilled his purpose in bringing his people to a degree of deliverance from the Philistine oppression. And even then, he died in the process!

Samson had no children, at least none that are recorded in the Bible. He was a "terminal generation." And if we don't do what we must do, we will find ourselves the parents of a terminal generation. There will be only increased misery and pain as we watch our children be destroyed and killed.

LEAVING AN INHERITANCE

The Bible tells us that a good man leaves an inheritance to his children, and to his children's children. (See Proverbs 13:22.) What you do goes beyond the next generation and then on to the next generation after that. As you train up your child, keep in mind always that you are building an inheritance for your grandchild!

God desires for each generation to go to a new level of glory in Him. We are to build on the best of the last generation, going to higher and higher levels of faith, understanding more and more about God's Word, and being more and more effective in God's kingdom.

The "passing" of the torch of faith occurs through "headship." It follows in the wake of the lineage of Abraham and Isaac and Jacob. The problem we are experiencing today is that in many communities, we have stopped the "passing on." We no longer are launching our children to an even higher level of faith in God.

My sons are *supposed* to do even greater works than I do. I am to build a platform on which they will rise up and engage in even greater spiritual warfare and trust the Lord to accomplish even greater things through their lives. But if I poison my children while they are at home with me, they will spend most of their lives trying to undo that poison and therefore, they will not become or be able to do all that God desires for them to become and to do.

If you really stop to think about it, you'll have to admit that the entire story of Christianity is the story of a Father and His Son. God the Father passed on Himself to His Son, Jesus Christ. The Son passed on Himself through the Holy Spirit so we might be joint heirs with Jesus Christ — sons and daughters of the Most High God.

You were saved and forgiven and came into a relationship with God because a Son was willing to be submissive to His Father.

You are blessed today because a Son did His Father's will and, even now, is seated at the Father's right hand to act as mediator and defender of those who believe in Him.

You experience God's love today because a Son experienced His Father's unconditional and eternal love.

You have the hope of eternal life today because a Father sent His Son to this earth to die for your sins, and that Son willingly obeyed His Father.

God intends for us, in turn, to pass on everything we know about having faith in Him to the next generation, so they can pass it on, pass it on, pass it on. And in that way, the kingdom of God is built and expands and deepens and strengthens. The blessing gets greater and greater, and the future is far more glorious than the past!

CONCLUSION:

VISIONS DO NOT COME TO PASS WITHOUT PAIN

If you want the fullness of God's blessing in your life, your marriage, and your family, you will be stretched. Anyone who ever achieved something great had to stretch for it. Failure comes when we shrink away from the challenge of being stretched. As long as we are willing to change in the ways God is calling us to change, God will be with us to help us.

Say to yourself often as you seek to obey and to do what God has put before you as His plan — "I'm going through because God is with me and He cannot be defeated." Don't shrink away from the challenge. Run toward it, not away from it!

If you don't move forward in the Lord, you move backwards. The same is true for your marriage and your family life. If you aren't moving forward, you are going to slide backwards. The momentum is in one direction or the other.

When you allow yourself to be stretched so you can come to a new and higher level of blessing, you are going to feel vulnerable. You may feel pain. You may be rejected by people whom you thought cared for you and were willing to be stretched along with you. Most people do not want to be stretched by God and don't allow themselves to be stretched by God. Therefore, when you allow yourself to be stretched, you are going against the norm.

Don't give up. Don't let yourself get discouraged. God will heal you of any pain you feel. He will restore to you what rejection and loneliness may try to eat away. He will give you a reputation of integrity and value, and He will give credibility to your witness.

BE WILLING FOR GOD TO CHANGE YOU

God has a transformation process ahead for each one of us.

I beseech you therefore, brethren, by the mercies of God, that ye present your bodies a living sacrifice, holy, acceptable unto God, which is your reasonable service.

And be not conformed to this world: but be ye transformed by the renewing of your mind, that ye may prove what is that good, and acceptable, and perfect, will of God.

Romans 12:1,2

God has a higher ideal in mind for us than we have in mind for ourselves. He has in mind for us what is good, acceptable, and perfect according to His plan. Our job is to be conformed to His higher ideal, to present ourselves to Him as if we are giving our entire lives as a sacrifice. When we do our part in obedience, He does His part in transformation.

We have to be willing to be changed by God, but if we are willing, He'll do the changing!

God's desire is to restore your femininity to you as a woman, to restore your masculinity to you as a man — and to do so in a way that will allow you to live in and fulfill His plan for your life. You won't be losing anything by becoming the woman God wants you to be or the man God wants you to be. Just the opposite! You'll gain. You'll feel fulfilled. You'll see progress and growth and development in your life. You'll come to a greater inner peace than that which you've ever known. God's plan is not to hurt us, harm us, or diminish us, but to enrich, enlarge, and bless us!

CHOOSE TO WALK BY FAITH, NOT BY SIGHT

Don't let what you see cause you to worry. Sometimes people start imagining all sorts of problems because they see or don't see certain things. They live their lives according to the "signs" of the day. That happened to Elisha's servant in 2 Kings 6. The servant got up one morning, went to the city wall, and saw that the city below him was surrounded by horses and chariots. He panicked and said to Elisha, **Alas, my master! how shall we do?** (2 Kings 6:15).

Elisha prayed and asked God to help his servant see the hidden things he couldn't see with his physical eyes. He prayed, **Lord, I pray thee, open his eyes, that he may see** (2 Kings 6:17). The Lord answered that prayer and the servant suddenly saw that the mountains were filled with horses and chariots of fire — an angelic host that far outnumbered the physical foe.

Many of us need to ask God to open our eyes to the bigger picture in the spirit realm. We need to see things as God sees them, not as we see things only with our physical eyes and our fleshly desires. Many things we think are challenges and troubles may actually be blessings when seen from God's standpoint — and that includes the troubles you might see in your marriage.

You may think your marriage is outside God's will because it is such a difficult marriage. God's Word to you is the same as His Word to Paul, who prayed to be released from a "thorn in the flesh" — a painful situation that caused Paul much discomfort and misery. God's Word is this: **My grace is sufficient** (2 Corinthians 12:9). If you will submit your painful marriage to God, He will do for you what He did for Paul. He will be your strength in that marriage and His grace will be sufficient for you to obtain the victory. He will show you the big picture.

God will be there with you even if your spouse is out on the town.

God will not turn His back on you or reject you even if your spouse does.

God will love you even if your spouse doesn't.

God will be available to you at three o'clock in the morning even if your spouse isn't there with you.

God will hear you every time you pray, and He will respond to you in compassion and with a good purpose, even if your spouse doesn't hear a word you say.

God will express His love to you all the way through your problem, trial, weakness, or difficulty until you emerge on the other side of it and begin to experience the fullness of His blessings.

The "troubles" you are experiencing in your marriage may actually be the entry point into a much deeper and more fulfilling relationship with God and your spouse. Trust Him. Walk with Him by faith. If He hasn't yet revealed to you how things will be when you emerge from your troubles, trust Him that things are going to be better because God is *always* in the process of working all things toward your greater good. (See Romans 8:28.)

GOD'S PERFECT ORDER

Is it possible to experience God's perfect order after the fall of Adam and Eve? Absolutely! The Bible gives us example after example. The words "repent," "rebirth," "restore," and "recover" occur again and again in the Word of God. The death and resurrection of Jesus made it possible for every person to return to a state of restoration with God and to live in full agreement with God's plan. Once we are saved and filled with God's Spirit, we are back to Genesis 1:1, **In the beginning God....** All of our life is back to that reality — God is supreme, He is the beginning of every future moment of our existence.

If we have made mistakes in our marriage, then we must repent together as man and wife and come again to that point of new beginning. We come back to the, **In the beginning God....** reality and confess to Him, "We need You. We are trusting You to work in our lives, in our marriage, and in our family. Forgive us and help us to start anew."

The only things that will be sustained by the power of God are those things which are ordained by God, started by God, and operate in obedience to God.

Did God ordain marriage for men and women? Yes.

Was God present when you and your spouse married? Yes.

Now it's up to you to walk in obedience to God and trust Him to sustain you, your marriage, and your family by His power.

God is the Alpha and the Omega — the beginning and the ending. He is the author and finisher. (See Revelation 22:13 and Hebrews 12:2.) Yes, there is a price to pay for establishing His order in your individual life, in your marriage, and in your children — but the way He finishes things out is far beyond our imagining!

Ask anyone who has paid this price, and I guarantee you they will say it was worth every bit of pain and perseverance to see their vision of a godly marriage and family become reality. They will point to their children, grandchildren, and great-grandchildren — who know, love, and serve God; who are world-changers and powerful witnesses for Jesus Christ — and they will have tears of joy in their eyes as they answer, "Absolutely. It was worth the price to obtain such a precious, eternal reward as this."

I pray you will know that same precious, eternal reward!

I pray you will have God's plan for your life, your marriage, and your family for generations to come.

Most of all, I pray you will know that no matter where you are right now, God's plan for your life — which is always the best — *can be yours!*

ABOUT THE AUTHOR

Bishop Eddie L. Long is God's visionary for New Birth Cathedral, located in Lithonia, Georgia. Serving as pastor since 1987, his consistent obedience to God has taken the New Birth congregation from glory to glory. The membership has grown from 300 in 1987 to 25,000 and counting. During these years, Bishop Long's uncompromising and bold teaching of God's word has changed the lives of people both at New Birth and around the world.

To accommodate the tremendous growth of church membership, several building expansion plans have been realized under the direction of Bishop Long. From the 500-seat chapel in 1987, he built a 3700-seat sanctuary in 1991, a 5000-seat Family Life center in 1999, and a 10,500-seat complex will be complete in Spring 2001. With these and other community-empowering projects, Bishop Long continues to equip people in economics, leadership and business.

Educationally, Bishop Long has earned a bachelor's degree in Business Administration from North Carolina Central University and a Master's of Divinity degree from Atlanta's Interdenominational Theological Center. Also, he has been awarded honorary doctorate degrees from his undergraduate alma mater and from Beulah Heights Bible College of Atlanta, where he has taken and taught several courses.

Bishop Long has achieved many triumphs on local, national and international levels. Among other honors, his name has been listed among America's 125 most influential leaders; he received the 1999 Legacy Award from Big Brothers Big Sisters of Metro Atlanta;

and he received the Distinguished Leadership Award from the Urban League. He is the founder and CEO of Faith Academy, New Birth's school of excellence, and he serves as the Vice Chair of the Morehouse School of Religion Board of Directors. Bishop Long and his wife Vanessa are the proud parents of four children: Eric, Edward, Jared and Taylor. The couple has also served as surrogate parents for many other children in the church and community.

Bishop Long's powerful messages are available in a plethora of video and audio tape series. Some of his best selling series include "I Don't Want Delilah, I Need You," "The Spirit of Negativity and Familiarity" and "Kingdom Relationships." Such messages and many others are broadcast in more than 172 countries via television and radio programs. A unique education on the biblical mandate of male/female relationships is found in his book *I Don't Want Delilah, I Need You;* in his book, Taking Over, he challenges church tradition and complacency, explaining the authority of God's Kingdom on earth; and his daily devotional book, *Called to Conquer,* will encourage you in word and spirit.

Many are blessed through various conferences hosted by Bishop Long each year, and generations are changed because of his passion for mentoring youth, men and pastors. Through his ministry, people are discovering their destinies. Because of the favor on his life, Bishop Long has close relationships with key leaders in the religious, political and entertainment arenas; consequently, this humble servant is advancing the Kingdom of God in a whole new way.

BOOKS BY EDDIE LONG

I Don't Want Delilah, I Need You!
Thy Kingdom Come

You may contact Bishop Long
by writing him at:

New Birth Missionary Baptist Church
P. O. Box 1019
Lithonia, Georgia 30058

or at the ministry website:
www.kingdom@newbirth.org

Thank you for selecting a book from
BETHANY HOUSE PUBLISHERS

Bethany House Publishers is a ministry of Bethany Fellowship
International, an interdenominational, nonprofit organization
committed to spreading the Good News of Jesus Christ around
the world through evangelism, church planting, literature
distribution, and care for those in need. Missionary training is
offered through Bethany College of Missions.

Bethany Fellowship International is a member of the National
Association of Evangelicals and subscribes to its statement of
faith. If you would like further information, please contact:

Bethany Fellowship International
6820 Auto Club Road
Bloomington, MN 55438 USA